I've Heard That All My Life!

Familiar Expressions
From The Bible

Ellis Dillard Thompson

CSS Publishing Company, Inc., Lima, Ohio

I'VE HEARD THAT ALL MY LIFE!

All scripture quoted in this book is taken from the *King James Version of the Holy Bible*,
except where it is noted otherwise.
　　The inserted words within some of the scripture are to offer additional clarification
which is intended to help the reader's understanding.

Scriptures marked NKJV are from *The New King James Version*. Copyright © 1979,
1980, 1982, Thomas Nelson Inc., Publishers.

Scriptures marked NIV are taken from the *Holy Bible, New International Version*. Copyright © 1973, 1978, 1984, International Bible Society. Used by permission of Zondervan
Bible Publishers. All rights reserved.

Scriptures marked NRSV are from the *New Revised Standard Version of the Bible*, copyright 1989 by the Division of Christian Education of the National Council of the Churches
of Christ in the USA. Used by permission.

Scriptures marked TLB are taken from *The Living Bible* © 1971. Used by permission of
Tyndale House Publishers, Inc., Wheaton, IL 60189. All rights reserved.

Library of Congress Cataloging-in-Publication Data

Thompson, Ellis Dillard, 1924-
　　I've heard that all my life : familiar expressions from the Bible / Ellis Dillard Thompson.
　　　　p.　　cm.
　　ISBN 0-7880-1190-1 (pbk.)
　　1. Bible—Quotations.　　I. Title.
BS416.T48　　　　1998
220.6—dc21　　　　　　　　　　　　　　　　　　　　　　　　　　97-26641
　　　　　　　　　　　　　　　　　　　　　　　　　　　　　　　　　　CIP

This book is available in the following formats, listed by ISBN:
　　0-7880-1190-1　　Book
　　0-7880-1191-X　　IBM 3 1/2
　　0-7880-1192-8　　MAC
　　0-7880-1193-6　　Sermon Prep

PRINTED IN U.S.A.

For my grandchildren,
Katy, Kevin, and Kelly,
whose childlike faith
is an inspiration to me.

Familiar Expressions From The Bible

Foreword

The secularization of America is hardly disputable. The Christian faith, and especially the practical and sometimes organized approach to faith, are on the decline. And yet, many of the expressions which have found their way into our everyday speech have gained popularity and have become commonplace because they are found in the Bible. People who have very little regard for organized religion can be heard to use terms like "apple of my eye" and "blind leading the blind." In fact, many of these critics have been heard to use phrases like "holier than thou" and "hypocrite."

People in many walks of life use these expressions. Backporch philosophers would be impoverished if they did not have maxims such as "the patience of Job," "reaping what you sow," and "the ox is in the ditch." Sports commentators would have to find another idiom for "smoother than butter" or "go the second mile"; and political commentators would have to come up with something other than "scapegoat"   and "eye to eye."

I am so appreciative of E.D. Thompson's recent offering, *I've Heard That All My Life!*, for several reasons. First, E.D. reminds us that these expressions used in the Bible have gained wide usage in our everyday speech. Second, he reminds us that faith and religion are applicable to everyday living. The Bible contains much wisdom which has aided the average human being in daily struggles for thousands of years. That this wisdom is still in popular usage attests to its timeless value. Third, E.D. not only has gone to the effort to remind us of the biblical use of many of our popular idioms of speech, but he also has given us a refreshing and much-needed excursion into the practical application of the faith embedded in these maxims.

This book will be of interest to people who enjoy tracing the ancestry of our folklore; it will prove to be a wonderful tool for the preacher who is in search of a good illustration ("stiffnecked"); it will give valuable resource to the counselor who is searching for a solid solution to one of life's problems ("there is nothing new under the sun"); and it will give comfort to those who are troubled ("thorn in the flesh").

I have known E.D. Thompson for nearly a quarter of a century and am presently proud to be his pastor. I not only recommend this book; I also plan to use it quite often in my preparation for sermons and Bible study. Thank you, E.D.!

The Rev. Michael D. O'Bannon, Senior Pastor
Belle Meade United Methodist Church
Nashville, Tennessee

Introduction

In this book, over 150 familiar expressions used today are pulled out of the Bible and identified as to their location in the Bible. Usually, only one location of the expression is given. That Bible verse is quoted.

These expressions force the audience to understand more clearly how much humanity and folk wisdom are owed to the teachings of the Bible.

The comments on specific expressions are concise and to the point. Many of them are introduced with interesting and sometimes humorous anecdotes revealing how the expressions are used in our present daily lives.

These comments, written for a general audience, can be read from standpoints of entertainment, information, and inspiration.

The book is designed to be non-judgmental of others, and the explanations are kept accessible to those readers who might be turned off by sophisticated and elaborate commentaries.

It is intended that the book might inform, teach, inspire, and display information in a different context from what the reader has learned elsewhere. It is hoped that the book will lead people to a higher plane in their relationships with their Creator.

1

Expression: A little lower than the angels

Location: Psalm 8:5

Verse: For thou hast made him [human beings] a little lower than the angels, and hast crowned him [them] with glory and honor.

A grandfather was seeing his granddaughter to bed one night. The five-year-old asked her grandfather to tell her a story after the light was dimmed. The grandfather sat at the edge of his grand-daughter's bed in the dim and shadowy room and began to speak softly.

"Once upon a time there was a man in a village who was believed to be stealing sheep from the farms and then selling the sheep in another town.

"Soon, the man was caught and was turned over to the people for a trial. This man was found guilty of being a thief. After some time and several meetings, the village people decided that they would stamp on this man's forehead the letters *S* and *T* with ink that could not be erased. This would stand for 'sheep thief' and everyone would see him and know what he was.

"After the two letters were stamped on the thief's forehead, he was so embarrassed that he had to move to a distant town and try to start his life over.

"After a period of time, this same man turned his life around and became one of the finest citizens possible. He attended church, he showed love for others, and he helped people when they were in need. The people in this new town didn't know that the letters on his forehead meant that he had been a sheep thief.

"One day another little girl in this town asked her grandfather what the letters *ST* that were stamped on this man's forehead meant. Her grandfather thought for a moment, and, remembering the man's love for God and all the kind things this man had done, then said, 'I guess the letters must stand for *SAINT*.'   "

By this time in the dim light of the room, the little granddaughter was sound asleep. The grandfather looked down at the innocence of his beautiful granddaughter and said, "God made people just a little lower than the angels."

Psalm 8 in the Bible speaks of the great worth of human beings. We humans have the stamp of the Creator on us.

2

Expression: Alpha and Omega

Location: Revelation 1:8

Verse: I am Alpha and Omega, the beginning and the ending, saith the Lord, which is, and which was, and which is to come, the Almighty.

All of the company sales people gathered in the top floor conference room for a seminar. The seminar's purpose was to present a new investment program to the sales force. Everyone was enthusiastic to unveil the new program and receive instruction on how to present and sell this new product to clients.

The charismatic leader of the group put the sales staff at ease by saying, "Don't worry. We will take you step-by-step through this presentation and cover every point from alpha to omega."

Alpha and omega are the first and last letters of the Greek alphabet. This is like the English "A to Z." From an alphabet we make words. It is interesting to note that in the Bible Jesus Christ is called the "Word of God."

Revelation 1:8 communicates that God rules over all human history — from beginning to the end of everything.

3

Expression: The apple of my eye

Location: Proverbs 7:2

Verse: Keep my commandments, and live; and my law [guard my teachings] as the apple of thine eye.

Grandparents often can be heard telling others what great love they feel for a grandchild. The great warmth and love that is felt for the little one is beyond words. Even so, a grandparent's love is probably just a fraction of what God's love for us must be like.

New grandparents had been on a trip and had not seen their baby granddaughter for a few days. When they returned home and went to visit their daughter, son-in-law, and that beautiful grandbaby, they saw the little one lying on a pallet on the floor. Both the grandmother and grandfather immediately fell down on the floor beside her. The grandmother gazed with much joy into the face of God's newest creation in their family and she said to the little one, "You are the apple of my eye."

In biblical times, the pupil of an eye was thought to have a shape resembling an apple. Thus Proverbs 7:2 teaches us that concern for obedience to God should be just as immediate to us as caring for the pupil of our eye.

4

Expression: As a lamb to the slaughter

Location: Isaiah 53:7

Verse: He was oppressed, and he was afflicted, yet he opened not
his mouth: he is brought as a lamb to the slaughter....

In a post-season college football bowl game, the two teams
seemed to be so unevenly matched that the sportswriter wrote in
his column that a certain team was going to be like a lamb being
led to the slaughter.

Ironically, on the front page of the newspaper on that same day,
there was a story of some elderly people who has been taken in by
a shrewd con man with his slick sales pitch. These people had been
cheated out of their life's savings. The journalist simply described
the elderly people as being lambs led to the slaughter.

This is how we use this expression in our present-day culture.
From a biblical point of view the expression is found in the book
of Isaiah revealing prophecy of the coming of Jesus Christ.

5

Expression: As a thief in the night

Location: 1 Thessalonians 5:2

Verse: For yourselves know perfectly that the day of the Lord so cometh as a thief in the night.

The Bible says that there is nothing new under the sun. Great novelists say that there is no such thing as a "new" plot.

A distinguished professor of literature actually told his students that there are only seven possible plots in writing. He even went to the chalkboard and wrote them down. However, each listing had quite a few subheadings.

The professor went on to say that interest could be created in plots by offering surprise — the unexpected. He then said, "No one should know what is to happen. There must be surprise, suddenness, something unexpected. It must come as a thief in the night."

First Thessalonians was written between A.D. 50 and 51 by the apostle Paul from Corinth to the Christians in Thessalonica, Greece. Paul is reiterating in this verse what Jesus said in his own words when he was on earth.

The Bible teaches that no one will know when Jesus' second coming will take place. Even believers will be surprised. It will be sudden. It will be unexpected. God will intervene directly and dramatically in world affairs. This was predicted and discussed often in the Old Testament also. But no one knows when. The day of the Lord will come as a thief in the night. Paul says, "Be ready!"

6

Expression: As white as snow

Location: Isaiah 1:18

Verse: Come now, and let us reason together, saith the Lord: though your sins be as scarlet, they shall be as white as snow ...

The fashion designer advertises that the material which goes into her dresses is white as snow.

The laundry detergent salesman says that his company's soap powder gets clothes whiter than snow.

The department store sign over the bedding department says: "Our white sheets are the whitest."

The Bible also describes things as white as snow.

Historically, this writing in the book of Isaiah concerns the aftermath of the fall of the Northern Kingdom of the Israelites when the Assyrians had invaded Judah and had carried away a large part of its population. The Lord, through the prophet Isaiah, is calling on the people to repent of their sins, reform, cleanse themselves, and be forgiven.

In this passage, scarlet refers to blood that has stained the hands of sinners. We know this from reading Isaiah 1:15-21.

White is a powerful figurative description of the result of forgiveness.

7

Expression: Ask and you shall receive

Location: John 16:24

Verse: ... Ask, and ye shall receive, that your joy [happiness] may be full.

In a church school class, the teacher read some scripture which included this verse from the book of John.

A young boy smiled as the teacher read. The student immediately responded, "Good! Then I ask for a new bicycle to be parked in front of the church for me when I leave today." The teacher smiled and just about guaranteed him that it would not be there.

The student exclaimed, "But the scripture says ..."

The teacher abruptly cut him off and said, "Well, sometimes God's answer to our prayers is 'No!' The teacher realized that more information was needed to help this student's understanding.

The teacher continued, "I think that a child of God who strives to live according to God's will can expect God to answer prayer."

The teacher paused to think of what better help might be offered. This teacher then said, "When my son was very small, he stuck a rusty nail in his foot. I rushed him to the doctor because I knew that he needed a tetanus shot.

"When my son saw the needle in the doctor's hand, he began to scream, 'Daddy, Daddy!'

"My heart was about to break as I saw his tiny outstretched arms pleading, 'Help me, Daddy. Help me.'

"But I just had to stand there, because I knew that the shot was what was best for my son.

"It came to my mind that this was the same as in my life when I have called out to God, 'Father, help me.' But God has had to stand watching me with all the compassion in the world and do what was best for me.

"God, with his love and compassion, does indeed answer prayer."

8

Expression: A babel

Location: Genesis 11:9

Verse: Therefore is the name of it called Babel; because the Lord did there confound [confuse] the language of all the earth ...

What is a "babel"? Babel is the English word describing a scene of noise or confusion.

The Bible gives the account of Noah's descendants speaking one language. The people journeyed eastward from the mountains of Ararat to a fertile plain called Babylonia between the Tigris and the Euphrates rivers.

After a long period of time, the human race multiplied and developed skills to build a city. The people wanted to build a tower whose summit was believed to be the gateway to heaven — the realm of the gods. They were seeking self-glory instead of God's glory. So the Tower of Babel was built from sun-dried clay bricks with bitumen for mortar. Because of the people's pride and rebellion, God scattered the people and confused their language.

"Babhel" is the Hebrew name for Babylon, where the tower was built. The Hebrew word "balal" means to confuse, and it sounds like "babel." The English word "babel" means a confusion of sounds.

The word "babel" is present in the familiar Christmas carol, "It Came Upon The Midnight Clear." The words were written by Edmund H. Sears in 1849, and one of his stanzas includes, "And ever o'er its babel sounds the blessed angels sing."

9

Expression: A backslider

Location: Hosea 14:4

Verse: I will heal their backsliding [disloyalty], I will love them
freely: for mine anger is turned away from him [them].

Bob grew up in a wonderful family. The whole family went to
Sunday school and church. As a young person Bob committed his
life to the Lord. When one is a "born-again Christian," that person
is regenerated by the Spirit of God. That person is given a new
nature that has a capacity for God and longs to serve God.

At this new birth, the person gets a new nature. But the problem is that the person doesn't lose the old nature. Then there are
the two natures contending for priority in that life. This is the
struggle that the apostle Paul went through. He tells of it in the
Bible. All of us have this problem.

Over the years Bob allowed the world to play a big role in his
life. In Bob's own words, "I became a backslider."

Bob began to drink, and he ran up terrible bills with his gam-
bling. After adultery, lies, and two marriages, Bob could admit that
his backsliding had caused him great torment.

But it doesn't matter how far we have wandered, we can always go home. The illustration that Jesus uses is about the prodigal son, which we can read about in Luke 15:11-24.

Bob had accepted the Lord in his life many years before, and
he kept having the urge to "go home." Bob had the desire to get
back into the fellowship with God. I presume that the average un-
regenerate sinner wants to keep on living in sin. He or she likes it.
Pigs love to live and eat in pigpens. But the prodigal son wasn't
satisfied to stay there. He wanted to get out and go home.

The word "backslider" appears only one time in the King James
Version of the Bible, but there are many times that the words

"backsliding" and "backslidings" are used. An example is given from Hosea.

A backslider's life will reap what it sows. But remember, our Father is always waiting for us to come back home.

10

Expression: **Be sure your sin will find you out**

Location: Numbers 32:23

Verse: But if ye will not do so, behold [then take note], ye have sinned against the Lord: and be sure your sin will find you out.

As the old gentleman stared at the newspaper, he would often shake his head and let out a word or two in disgust as he read of the most recent murders, robberies, rapes, violence, and corruption.

Finally, he folded the newspaper and slammed it down on the empty chair beside him. Being a man of religion —   a man of the cloth — this aging preacher sighed, "Be sure your sin will find you out."

These words were spoken by Moses a few thousand years ago to some Israelites who made a certain request of him.

In the long journey with Moses leading the children of Israel out of Egypt to the Promised Land, just before crossing over the Jordan River they came upon a land which was good for livestock grazing. Some of the tribes of Israel requested to stay there and let this land be their inheritance.

Moses reprimanded them for not wanting to go on and help their people get across the Jordan to the Promised Land of Canaan.

But the tribes begged to stay and they promised that they would move on to help the children of Israel reach their inheritance beyond the River Jordan if they could be permitted first to build proper sheepfolds for their livestock and cities for their wives and little ones in this land of Gilead which they wanted.

Moses then agreed that if they would do that which they had promised and help their people move on, they could return to the land they wanted. Moses sternly informed them that if they did not keep their promise, "Be sure your sin will find you out."

11

Expression: Be ye doers and not hearers only

Location: James 1:22

Verse: But be ye doers of the Word, and not hearers only, deceiving [cheating] your own selves.

The newly-appointed pastor of the little country church was at home reading in the comfort of his favorite chair when his wife returned home from a meeting. The door opened, and she entered, saying, "Be ye doers and not hearers only." Her husband looked up and said with a smile, "Are you doing some memory work on your Bible verses?"

In a very exhausted manner, the pastor's wife sat down and began to tell about the committee meeting she had attended. Knowing the frustration of what some committee meetings might bring, her husband laughed and said, "Well, you know that expression which says, 'God so loved the world that he didn't send a committee!' "

The wife's frustration was evident as she began to tell the intricacies of the meeting during which people apparently were big talkers, but when it came to getting the job done, they were still just talkers.

Of course, her quoting of the Bible verse was quite appropriate. James is telling us not merely to listen to God's Word, but to do what it says.

12

Expression: **The blind leading the blind**

Location: Luke 6:39

Verse: ... Can the blind lead the blind? Shall they not both fall into the ditch?

A mother was distressed when she heard that her young daughter wanted to go visit a friend who lived across town. Knowing that her daughter was rather inexperienced in getting around town to places unfamiliar to her, the mother showed some stress when she said, "But how will you be able to get there and find her house?"

The daughter calmly responded, "Oh, it will be fine, because Sally is going with me."

The mother, realizing the inexperience of Sally also, showed even more stress as she blurted out, "That will be the blind leading the blind."

This, of course, was not the way to approach this matter. The mother did harm in implying to her daughter that she was not capable, and that she did not trust her.

Of course, we can understand the anxiety on the mother's part. There is so much meanness and evil on the streets now, it is perfectly understandable why a parent would have concern.

Jesus often taught his lessons in parables. In the book of Luke, Jesus is quoted as using this expression. Jesus wants us to follow the leaders who will guide us into trust and faith.

13

Expression: A born-again Christian

Location: John 3:3

Verse: ... Verily, verily [most assuredly], I say to thee, except a man [unless one] be born again [from above], he cannot [no one can] see the kingdom of God.

The expression "born again" is brought up on a great number of talk shows. Almost always either the talk show host or the guest will state, "Born again? I don't know what that means."

The Bible teaches that we are to be baptized by water and the Spirit. We are born as humans in the water of our mother's womb. We can be baptized with water in a ceremony performed by our church pastor. More importantly, the Bible often refers to water as symbolic of spreading the gospel message. This implies that to be born again, the holy Word of God must be applied to us by the Spirit of God. God's being made real to our heart by the Holy Spirit makes us a born-again Christian. Our lives are completely changed as though we have been "born again." We become new creatures (2 Corinthians 5:17).

John tells us about the night that a Jewish religious leader named Nicodemus came to talk with Jesus privately. Nicodemus was a Pharisee and a member of the Sanhedrin, which is like a city council. In the conversation with Nicodemus, Jesus spoke the above words to him.

The apostle Paul said in effect that when we are born again, Christ's love begins to control us.

Jesus said on that night to Nicodemus, and Jesus says to us, "Marvel not that I said unto thee, Ye must be born again" (John 3:7).

14

Expression: The bottomless pit

Location: Revelation 20:1-2

Verse: And I [John] saw an angel come down from heaven, having the key of the bottomless pit and a great chain in his [the angel's] hand. And he [the angel] laid hold on the dragon [Satan] ...

In the late 1940s, the movies from Hollywood began to depict many social problems which the public found interesting. For instance, the movie *Pinky* dealt with racial prejudice. Political corruption was discussed in such movies as *All The King's Men*. And the movie *The Snake Pit* was one of the first movies to deal with the mentally ill. This movie, based on the novel by Mary Jane Ward, featured many great actors whose names will be recognized by buffs of the Golden Age of Hollywood — such greats as Olivia de Havilland, Mark Stevens, Celeste Holm, Leif Erickson, and Beulah Bondi.

The sobering dramatics of this picture added the element of shock as the audience gazed down into the dark, deep pit filled with snakes. One could not see this without thinking of the phrase "the bottomless pit" found in the Bible.

In place of "bottomless pit," some Bible translations use the word "abyss." Abyss is a Greek word which actually means "very deep" or "bottomless."

This is part of a vision that John writes about in the book of Revelation which symbolizes an event where Satan, the major instigator of earth's evil, has to be dealt with by God.

15

Expression: Busybodies

Location: (see below)

Verse: (see below)

All of us can get a visual impression when we think of the word "busybodies." Meredith Wilson gives a wonderful musical picture of this in his musical, *The Music Man*. In the song, "Pick-a-little, Talk-a-little," the music generates the fast and furious busyness of the town gossips. In this musical this happens to be portrayed by ladies, but men are certainly not excluded from this behavior. God's Word speaks of what great damage this can cause.

The words "busybody" and "busybodies" are found exactly three times in the King James Version of the Bible:

1. For we hear that there are some which walk among you disorderly [living irresponsibly], working not at all, but are busybodies (2 Thessalonians 3:11).

2. And withal [in addition] they learn to be idle, wandering about from house to house; and not only idle, but tattlers [gossips] also and busybodies, speaking [repeating] things which they ought not (1 Timothy 5:13).

3. But let none of you suffer as a murderer, or as a thief, or as an evildoer, or as a busybody [meddler] in other men's [people's] matters (1 Peter 4:15).

In this last verse quoted, isn't it interesting that busybodies (meddlers and gossips) are mentioned right along with murderers?

16

Expression: By the skin of my teeth

Location: Job 19:20

Verse: My bone cleaneth [clings] to my skin and to my flesh, and I am escaped with [by] the skin of my teeth.

Some young people were hiking in the woods on a beautiful spring day. While enjoying the scenic wonders of nature, they decided to take a route that they had never traveled before. The beauty of the trees, the wild flowers, and the sounds of the birds were interrupted in a moment by the roar of a sliding boulder coming down the side of the mountain. The sound gave them the opportunity to run for an open area just in time. No one was hurt by what could have been disaster. The great sighs of relief were intruded on by one person's saying, "I escaped by the skin of my teeth."

In the Bible, Job was beset by many problems. He was engrossed in confusion. Then a burst of faith in God enlightened Job and lifted him out of the sadness of despair. Job expressed just how bad his situation was when he stated the words above.

17

Expression: Can the leopard change its spots?

Location: Jeremiah 13:23

Verse: Can the Ethiopian[s] change his [their] skin [color], or the leopard his [its] spots? Then may ye also do good, that are accustomed to do evil.

God, through the prophet Jeremiah, speaks to his people who are living a corrupt life and are in need of changing their way of living.

God is asking a rhetorical question. In their present state of being separated from God, the people could not change. Also, it is a truism that if we live less than acceptable lives for a long period of time, it gets harder and harder to reverse our style of living. In the New Testament, Jesus tells us that everyone who commits sin is a slave to sin (John 8:34).

In Jeremiah we read where God reveals the statement saying, "Return, ye backsliding children, and I heal your backslidings [faithlessness]" (Jeremiah 3:22). When this happens, the spots can be changed.

18

Expression: **Carved in stone**

Location: Deuteronomy 4:13

Verse: And he [God] declared unto you [Moses] his covenant [agreement], which he commanded you to perform [obey], even ten commandments; and he wrote them upon two tables [tablets] of stone.

It is not hard for us to believe in rules which are "carved in stone."

One of the Bible's most sacred accounts describes Moses receiving the ten commandments from God at Mount Sinai.

Moses stood at the foot of the mountain and gazed upon the fire with black clouds and deep darkness when he heard the Lord speak. Out of the fire Moses heard the sounds of words, but saw no form. There was only a voice. God gave to Moses the ten commandments and wrote them on two stone tablets.

Moses returned to his people from this encounter, carrying the two stone tablets with the commandments "carved in stone."

19

Expression: Cast the first stone

Location: John 8:7

Verse: ... He [anyone] that is without sin among you, let him [that person] first cast a stone at her.

Radio talk shows are filled with many callers who are quick to condemn others for immoral or illicit acts. If those callers' true hearts were left open for others to see, they too might be guilty of the same acts or worse. It would be appropriate to say to them, "All who are without sin, let them cast the first stone."

Once the religious leaders brought to Jesus a young woman who was an adulteress. She had been caught in the very act. During that time in history, it was the law to stone the guilty person to death. The religious leaders asked Jesus what they should do. They were trying to trap Jesus so that they could accuse Jesus of doing something wrong.

But Jesus just stooped down and wrote in the dirt as though he had not heard them. When they continued to ask him, Jesus lifted himself up and spoke the words above.

Then everyone slowly moved away from the scene until finally the woman and Jesus were the only two left there. When Jesus saw none others present, he said to the woman, "Go and sin no more."

20

Expression: Charity begins at home

Location: 1 Timothy 5:4

Verse: ... Let them learn first to show piety [their religious practice including charity] at home, and to requite [repay] their parents: for that is good and acceptable before God.

Years ago our next-door neighbors were an elderly mother and her daughter. The elderly lady was in very poor health. I was always impressed with the sweet, gentle nature of both of these ladies. The daughter took loving care of her mother; she never got impatient with her mother and didn't mind at all in helping her to dress, eat, walk out to the porch, or adjust the television set. They were two who always displayed God's love through their lives.

After a while, my family moved away. My wife kept in touch with these old neighbors by telephone, and we visited them on occasion. We visited in their home just a short time before this elderly mother passed away.

The next Christmas we went to visit the daughter to take her a gift and see how she was doing. We saw the same beautiful, loving, and caring person. Nothing had changed about her except that now "Mama was no longer there."

This wonderful daughter told us that she had given up some things concerning her own life but had gained many other wonderful things by caring for her mother. Following God's way brought her much happiness.

Charity beginning at home is taught to us by the apostle Paul in the First Epistle to Timothy. Paul encouraged Timothy to teach his congregational members right standards and values. Paul taught that a Christian who would not support and care for his own dependents was worse than an unbeliever.

Chapter five of First Timothy stresses that we should be respectful to our elders as though they were our parents, to treat young

34

people as we would our brothers and sisters, and to care for those who have lost their spouses. Verse four states that members of the family should take the responsibility of caring for parents. Yes, kindness and charity begin at home.

21

Expression: Children of God

Location: John 1:12 (NRSV)

Verse: But to all who received him [Christ], who believed in his name, he gave power [the right] to become children of God.

It was a week before Christmas. I took some garbage out to our trash cans and saw a note attached to one of the containers. The note was from the weekly collector of our trash who was wishing us a Merry Christmas. The message also contained other printed phrases from his company which implied that a gift of cash would be appreciated.

I placed some cash in a Christmas card and wrote a short message which was something like this:

> *We wish for you and yours a very special Christmas and God's richest blessings. May God shower blessings on each of us for the coming year. God's love and peace for all of us. Merry Christmas, The Thompsons.*

About a week later, I was driving down our driveway when I saw the waste disposal company truck. The man driving the truck stopped quickly and ran over to my car. I rolled my window down so I could speak to him.

In a very timid and humble manner, this worker said, "I want to thank you for the Christmas gift, but mainly I want to thank you for that card."

I responded, "You are certainly welcome."

He went on to say, "The words that you put on that Christmas card treated me like a person of importance rather than just a garbage collector. You said that you asked for God to bless all of us. You included me."

After a few more words we parted and I drove on. I reflected on what he had just said. All of us are equal in the eyes of God. The Bible refers to all believers as "children of God."

I have no way to know whether that man is a child of God or not. I do not know what is in his heart. However, by the way he expressed himself and the interest he had in the care of God, I have strong feelings that he too is one of the children of God.

22

Expression: **Choose your friends carefully**

Location: Proverbs 12:26 (NKJV)

Verse: The righteous should choose his [your] friends carefully [be cautious], for the way of the wicked leads them astray.

A teacher of 25 years often enjoyed reflecting on the diversity of the hundreds of students he had taught over the years. Each student had his or her own personality and character traits. He remembered a young lady who came over to his desk on registration day one year and paid him a very high compliment. She said, "In being around you today, I have noticed that the students like you and can depend on what you say."

This teacher recalled that he was totally dumbfounded but definitely flattered. After thanking her for the unsolicited adulation, he listened as she continued.

"I am new in town and my friends told me to be very careful who I choose as my friends."

That, of course, was excellent advice. Then she proceeded to ask about a certain girl she had met. The teacher was delighted to tell her that she had chosen one of the nicest, friendliest, and most caring young ladies in the school. He told her she had made a good choice in choosing this girl as a new friend.

Adults have always told young people to "choose your friends carefully, and don't take up with the wrong crowd." People realize that running with the wrong crowd can help lead a good person astray. This wisdom is found in the Bible.

Marian Wright Edelman, in her book *The Measure of our Success*, writes: "Choose your friends carefully ... You were born God's original. Try not to become someone's copy."

23

Expression: Count the cost

Location: Luke 14:28 (NKJV)

Verse: For which of you, intending to build a tower, does not sit down first and count [estimate] the cost, whether he [one] has enough to finish it.

If we want to remodel a house, build a deck over the carport, or build a shelf, we first sit down and do what my father used to say. His remark was, "We will have to put the pencil to it." We knew that we had to figure exactly how it would be done, what materials the job would take, and how much money it would cost. In other words, we had to count the cost.

In the book of Luke we read where Jesus spoke to the large crowds about counting the cost of discipleship.

The Bible in this section of scripture is telling us to keep our word — to count the cost before we speak. Don't make a vow until we are certain we can keep it.

24

Expression: Deaf as an adder

Location: Psalm 58:4

Verse: ... they are like the deaf adder that stoppeth her ear.

There was a lovely old couple that everyone enjoyed being around. Their jokes and laughter had a way of making everyone feel good. The evidence of love they had for each other played a great role in lending happiness to others.

Whenever the wise old gentleman didn't want to respond with an answer, he had a way of evading the question. Then his dear, loving wife would say, "Oh, when he doesn't want to answer you, he is deaf as an adder."

An adder is a venomous serpent like a cobra. An ancient Oriental belief taught that the adder was able to stop up its hearing with the tip of its tail, and thereby not be charmed by the music of the snake charmers.

The analogy in the Bible is that the wicked have a way of shutting off the voice of righteousness.

25

Expression: A dog returns to its vomit

Location: Proverbs 26:11

Verse: As a dog returneth to his [its] vomit, so a fool returneth [reverts] to his [or her] folly.

Some of us never seem to learn. We keep going back and making the same mistakes time after time.

There was a very stern boss who would say to his employees, "Everyone makes mistakes, but don't let me see you make the same mistake twice."

When this boss was asked to give a recommendation for a past employee, his response was a little different from what was expected. His statement was, "Some people work five years and get five years' experience. This fellow you are asking about worked five years and got one year's experience five times."

All have observed how a dog will return to its vomit. This is repulsive and sickening to see, but it is a truism. The Bible gives this very harsh analogy to the fool who hasn't learned a thing and will return to the folly of sin.

Peter in his Second Epistle presents this proverb characterizing the hypocrites. In very vivid language Peter describes the hypocrite like a dog, as well as like the sow being washed and then going right back to wallow in the mud (2 Peter 2:22).

26

Expression: Don't hide your light under a bushel

Location: Matthew 5:15

Verse: Neither do men [people] light a candle [lamp], and put it under a bushel [basket], but on a candlestick [lampstand]; and it giveth light unto all that are in the house.

The high school band was one of the splendid showpieces in this town of about 40,000. Along with the picturesque lake, the majestic bridge, and some fine old homes, the band was a source of pride.

During a summer concert in the park, the band played an arrangement by one of the talented band students. No one knew that this student had the ability to create such a fine musical work. After the selection was performed and the energetic applause died down, the school's band director stepped to the microphone and congratulated the student arranger. Then the director added, "We didn't know you could write band arrangements like that. You must write some more and let us play them. Don't hide your light under a bushel."

This scripture means that people are to witness for good, and be a light for others to see and follow.

27

Expression: **Don't let the sun go down on your anger**

Location: Ephesians 4:26

Verse: ... let not the sun go down upon your wrath [anger].

The telephone rang while I was sitting with my church pastor in his study. My pastor picked up the phone and said, "Hello, may I help you?" From this point on, the tone of the pastor's voice clearly revealed that he had a very distraught and troubled person on the telephone. I motioned to my pastor that I would leave and see him later.

My pastor was saying many things while I tried to get my coat and belongings together. He was trying to calm and comfort this person on the phone.

As I left through the door of the study, I heard my pastor say, "Don't let the sun go down on your anger." My heart smiled at such an expression. We find this very meaningful expression in the book of Ephesians.

28

Expression: Don't worry about tomorrow

Location: Matthew 6:34 (NRSV)

Verse: So do not worry about tomorrow, for tomorrow will bring
worries of its own. Today's trouble is enough for today.

As a young child, I can remember what my church school
teacher told us about Jesus caring for us. It made a real impression
on me when this dear, graying, wrinkled, but attractive lady spoke
to us. Her voice seemed to have a calming effect.

I remember the lesson in which she explained that Jesus knows
every time a sparrow falls, and how much more important we are
to him. She told us that God knows the number of hairs on our
heads. She explained that if God cares for the birds and flowers,
we must know that God cares for us, too. She convinced us that if
our own mother and father love us and care for us, just how much
more our Heavenly Father must care for and love us.

This dear church school teacher then straightened to a more
erect posture and pushed her arms out in front of her as she said,
"So, don't worry about tomorrow!" I have never forgotten that.

In the sixth chapter of the book of Matthew, verses 25 through
34, are the actual spoken words of Jesus as he says,   "Do not worry
Jesus tells us not to worry about our lives, what we will eat or
drink or with what we will be clothed. Look at the birds of the air.
The Heavenly Father feeds them. Look at the lilies of the field.
Our Father clothes them in beautiful splendor. Yes, God can carry
us through all of our guilts and burdens, too.

Making plans for tomorrow is time well spent; worrying about
tomorrow is time well wasted.

29

Expression: **Dot every "i" and cross every "t"**

Location: Matthew 5:17-18

Verse: Think not that I am come to destroy [abolish] the law, or the prophets: I am not come to destroy [abolish], but to fulfill. For verily I say unto you, till heaven and earth pass, one jot* or one tittle** [dot of the "i" or cross of the "t"] shall in no wise pass from the law, till all be fulfilled [accomplished].

My wife and I recently paid a visit to a lawyer to get some legal help with regard to some real estate we own. The lawyer seemed quite efficient and told us that he would research every aspect of the matter. As we stood up to leave his office, his final statement was, "Don't worry, I will take real good care of the matter. I shall dot every 'i' and cross every 't.' " I like a person like that.

I am proud to say that our son possesses this type of meticulous correctness. When I ask him to do a job of some kind for me, I am able to forget about it completely and know that he will carry out the duties with his capable accuracy and his competent organizational skills. I know that he will dot every "i" and cross every "t."

God's Word expresses this thought in revealing that Jesus came to this earth not to abolish but to fulfill the law of the Old Testament.

Jesus fulfilled the Law during his earthly stay through his sinless, holy life and his sacrificial death. God gave us a way to inherit eternal life. Jesus Christ was our lamb that sacrificed himself on the cross. The way we can fulfill the Law is by accepting and living for the One who could fulfill it — Jesus Christ.

---

* Jot is the smallest Hebrew letter.
** Tittle is the minute ornament over a Hebrew letter

30

Expression: Down to the sea in ships

Location: Psalm 107:23-24

Verse: They that go down to the sea in ships, that do business in great waters; these see the works of the Lord, and his wonders in the deep.

The sailor holding watch on his ship late at night felt lonely. However, this feeling was soon abandoned as he began to direct his thinking to the beauty around him.

The sailor observed the vastness of the open sea. He watched the power of the rhythmic waves and thought that no human hand could reach down and hold them back. The white water crest behind the ship was a painting on the horizon. The moonlight stretched across the water for miles. All of it was under a great canopy of stars. This sailor was observing the power of God in action.

Soon after, in a letter to his mother back home, the sailor related some of these feelings. He ended his letter by telling his mother that he had been made aware that God could also still the waves and calm the storm in his life. He then signed the letter, "With love, your son." We can imagine what a wonderful effect this had on his mother, who also sometimes felt that loneliness and anxiety.

31

Expression: A drop in the bucket

Location: Isaiah 40:15

Verse: Behold, the nations [all the people in the world] are as a drop of [in] a bucket, and are counted as the small dust of the balance [on the scales]....

The local community club was on a campaign to raise money for a recreation center for the youth. After the first day of campaigning, the club had raised only a tiny fraction of what was needed. The response was, "What we collected is just a drop in the bucket."

You can realize just how small one drop of water is in a large bucket. It is very tiny. It would take a very large amount of drops to create any significant filling of that bucket.

This text is saying that God is incomparable to anything. God's power and promises will not fail. All else is as a drop in the bucket.

32

Expression: Ears shall tingle

Location: 2 Kings 21:12

Verse: ... Behold, I am bringing such evil [disaster] upon Jerusalem and Judah, that whosoever heareth of it, both his [one's]
ears shall tingle.

During the reign of Manasseh over the land of Judah around
696-642 B.C., apostasy was alive and well. Apostasy is the falling
away by the people from the true gospel. History tells us some of
the people's ways of apostasy. They worshiped idols instead of the
one true God. There were wildly licentious dances, snake worship,
male and female prostitutes, planetary worship, human sacrifices,
and demon-inspired occultism. So God sent his Word to the people
through his prophets.

In other words, the news that the people would hear would be
utterly astonishing. The news would make their ears tingle.

33

Expression: Eat, drink, and be merry

Location: 1 Corinthians 15:32 (TLB)

Verse: ... then we might as well go and have ourselves a good
time: let us eat, drink, and be merry. What's the difference?
For tomorrow we die, and that ends everything.

The young man walking out to get into his car yelled back to
his two colleagues standing in the parking lot, "Tonight let's eat,
drink, and be merry."

How often have we heard people speak this expression? Some,
I fear, say this almost as a means of justifying some of their actions.
The apostle Paul spoke those words in a much different context.

The First Epistle to the Corinthians was written to the people
of the church in Corinth, Greece, by Paul while he was in Ephesus.
Corinth was a cosmopolitan center widely known for its immoral
behavior. It was known for its drunken parties, cheating, fornica-
tion, adultery, and other immoral acts.

In the fifteenth chapter of First Corinthians, Paul is strenuously
trying to convince the people about the Good News and saving
power of Jesus Christ. He is trying to save them for eternal life.
Paul is saying that if the dead will not have life again, then what is
the point of being baptized? He asks why we do many other things
in the name of God if it is only for some gain in our lives here on
earth. Paul says that if we will never live again in eternal life, then
we might as well eat, drink, and be merry!

34

Expression: **The eleventh hour**

Location: Matthew 20:6

Verse: And about the eleventh hour he went out, and found others standing idle....

The eleventh hour is referred to as being the last possible time to make a decision or take some kind of action.

The radio announcer reported on a serious vote before Congress: "Everyone had ears to the radio anxiously awaiting a decision by Congress on this important issue. Sure enough, the matter came to a vote, but it was right down to the eleventh hour."

In biblical times, the "sixth hour" is like our noon; the "ninth hour" is 3:00 p.m.; and the "eleventh hour" is 5:00 p.m.

This scripture is part of Jesus' parable about the workers in the vineyard. Some laborers were hired to work at the eleventh hour, and the workers hired much earlier in the day were upset that they made the same wages. The parable is Jesus' way of teaching that God's salvation can come to all, even at the eleventh hour.

35

Expression: **Everyone has a cross to bear**

Location: Luke 9:23

Verse: ... If any man [person] will come after me, let him deny himself [put aside one's own desires], and take up his [or her] cross daily, and follow me.

I was seated in a restaurant reading the morning newspaper. Two gentlemen came in and sat at the table next to me. Their conversation revealed quite a bit about each of their lives. I was not trying to be an eavesdropper. In fact, I would have been much happier if I could have concentrated on my morning newspaper. But when you are only thirty inches away from someone, it is impossible not to hear him speak.

One of the gentlemen began to talk about his child who had been diagnosed with cancer. His voice revealed the torment he was feeling. If this were not bad enough, the other gentleman began telling about his son who he was afraid was on drugs.

Finally, I heard one of the men say, "Well, I guess everyone has a cross to bear." Not a truer statement could have been spoken by this man. This expression about the cross comes straight from the Bible. However, Jesus' use of this expression, "bearing your cross," has to do with committing our lives to God's laws of values, morals, goals, and purposes.

The first mention of the cross is in the Gospel according to Saint Matthew (Matthew 10:38). The cross was an instrument of death in the Roman tradition. Criminals were to carry their own crosses to their executions. The cross symbolizes the necessity of total commitment — even unto death.

36

Expression: **Faith can move mountains**

Location: 1 Corinthians 13:2

Verse: ... and though I have all faith, so that I could remove [move] mountains, and have not charity [love], I am nothing.

Have you ever heard the expression that if you have a big job to be done, give it to the busiest person? It seems that the busy people have the talent and drive to take on even another job and get it done.

Miss Ellie in our church was like that. People said of Miss Ellie, "Give the task to her. She can move mountains."

Paul doesn't literally mean to displace a mountain of soil. Paul uses the hyperbole to express a special capacity to have faith in God to meet all needs.

Whatever troubles, guilts, sorrows, or other mountains we have to face in life, God has promised throughout his Word, the Bible, that we can expect God's help through faith. As it is written in the book of Matthew: "... If ye have faith ... ye shall say unto this mountain, Remove [move] hence ... and it shall remove [move]; and nothing shall be impossible unto you" (Matthew 17:20).

37

Expression: **The fat of the land**

Location: Genesis 45:18

Verse: And take your father and your households, and come unto me: and I will give you the good of the land of Egypt, and ye shall eat the fat of the land.

Joseph, who wore the coat of many colors, was rejected, kidnapped, enslaved, and imprisoned by his brothers. However, Joseph forgave them and shared his prosperity with them. The analogy is that God forgives and showers goodness on his people, too.

Joseph was made overseer of Egypt by Pharaoh. There came a great famine in the land where Joseph's father and eleven brothers were. Joseph welcomed his father and brothers in Egypt, where he could help them survive.

Pharaoh himself said that he would assign to them the very best territory in the land of Egypt, which was called the land of Goshen. He told them that they would live off "the fat of the land."

38

Expression: **The fear of the Lord**

Location: Job 28:28

Verse: And unto man [humanity] he said, Behold, the fear [respect] of the Lord, that is wisdom; and to depart from evil is understanding.

Of all the expressions in this book, probably the one you have heard more often than any other is "the fear of the Lord." This has been used in a multitude of contexts and is probably one of the most misunderstood phrases.

The excited tourist was telling about his ride in the cable car over the gigantic whirlpool near Niagara Falls. He concluded by saying, "That will put the fear of the Lord in you."

The television news reported the heinous crime by a criminal, and the viewer exclaimed, "What he needs is the fear of the Lord put in him."

It seems that everyone wants to teach others to have the fear of the Lord.

A common dictionary probably will define "fear" with words describing the idea of being apprehensive or afraid of something. But this does not adequately explain what is truly meant by "the fear of the Lord."

Those who fear the Lord are those who honor God, trust God, and order their lives in accordance with God's will because of their reverence for God.

Think of the word "fear" as denoting awe and reverence for God. It represents respect for God's loftiness and power and our dependence on God as our Creator. We should not think of fear as representing a cringing dread.

When we can truly "fear" our Lord — revere, respect, honor, trust, and obey — we can have an eternal relationship with God.

39

Expression: Feet of clay

Location: Daniel 2:34 (NIV)

Verse: While you are watching, a rock was cut out, but not by human hands. It struck the statue on its feet of iron and clay and smashed them.

No person wants the expression "feet of clay" said concerning one's self. It is human nature to want to be respected, admired, honored, and loved.

This expression was used just recently about a politician. This lawmaker was not respected. He was easily swayed, could not stand up for a conviction, and even was led into criminal acts and corruption. He had feet of clay. This is a horrible assessment of a person.

Nebuchadnezzar, who served as king of Babylon from the year 606 until 561 B.C., had a dream of an awesome image. The image's head was made of gold, its chest and arms were made of silver, its belly and thighs were made of bronze, its legs were made of iron, and its feet were made partly of iron and partly of clay. In his dream a stone fell and crushed the feet to pieces, thus destroying the image.

Young Daniel, the prophet, received a vision from God during the night which gave the interpretation of the king's dream. Daniel explained to the mighty king that he, Nebuchadnezzar, represents this head of gold. The other metals represent future kingdoms. The feet of iron and clay represent a kingdom that will be partly strong and partly fragile. The stone, which is the Kingdom of God to come, will crush all of the other kingdoms and will stand forever.

We can be thankful that the Kingdom of God will overcome the world and will live for all eternity.

40

Expression: Fight the good fight

Location: 1 Timothy 6:12

Verse: Fight the good fight of faith, lay hold on [deliberately seek] eternal life....

The football team lost the game. The damp, cold night hung around the lights of the stadium as the team carried the same emotional dreariness into the locker room. After a few moments of silence, the coach simply said, "We were overpowered, but thanks to you young men, we were able to fight the good fight."

That may be the way we would use this expression today, but First Timothy speaks of something far more profound. Paul in his letter to Timothy is speaking of keeping the faith.

Paul is saying to fight the good fight — enter into spiritual conflict against worldly things — the good fight of faith.

41

Expression: **A fool is right in one's own eyes**

Location: Proverbs 12:15

Verse: The way of a fool is right in his [one's] own eyes: but he [the one] that hearkeneth [heeds] unto counsel [advice] is wise.

There was a young man in the community who had joined a religious cult of some sort. He put down anyone who was a Christian. People did not try to preach to him, but often someone would indulge him in conversation.

This young man constantly threw out phrases such as: "I'm all right," "What's wrong with me?" "I'm an honest man," and "I do good things for people."

This young man seemed to be all right in his own eyes. But he was missing so much due to the lack of counseling from wise people and from faith in the wisdom of God.

There was one occasion when a neighbor put his arm around the young man and used the expression, "Why don't you let go and let God."

In this verse from Proverbs, the "he" is referring to Rehoboam, the son of Solomon. Rehoboam refused the wise counsel of the older ones in his kingdom, which resulted in his own downfall and civil war in his nation.

We who heed counsel are wise.

42

Expression: Forget the past

Location: Philippians 3:13

Verse: ... but this one thing I do, forgetting those things which are behind [in the past], and reaching forth [forward] unto those things which are before [ahead].

The apostle Paul wrote a letter to the people of Philippi around the year 61 A.D. while he was imprisoned in Rome. Even in prison Paul's faith endured, and he was determined to serve God and to teach others.

It was in this letter that Paul wrote the famous words of truth: "I can do all things through Christ who strengthens me" (Philippians 4:13). Paul relied on Christ for his abiding strength. In this letter, Paul wrote also the words in the verse above.

Of course, we realize that we are not to forget the past in every way. We must live up to what we have already attained. Our knowledge is to carry us on. We are able to profit from our past experience. But Paul is saying that he is pressing forward to an even higher calling.

We must realize that as children of God we are forgiven for our past sins. We need to move on to a higher calling in a life of faith and obedience because of our hope in God.

43

Expression: **Freely you have received, so freely give**

Location: Matthew 10:8

Verse: Heal the sick, cleanse the lepers, raise the dead, cast out devils: freely ye have received, freely give.

Jesus sent the twelve apostles out endued with miraculous powers to teach and preach to the people. Their commission was to confirm the gospel of the kingdom with these powers.

I remember a person I met during the early 1990s. The place was a mission house in a large metropolitan city which was dedicated to helping homeless street people.

A man who was serving as a volunteer at the mission freely gave of his time to cook, clean, open the mail, and do just about anything that came along that needed to be done.

It was later learned that this volunteer at one time had lost his job, and his wife and son had been killed in a car wreck. He had no other family. For a time he depended on this mission house for his meals and his life. He expressed that he was thankful that he had freely received, so now he would freely give.

Great happiness and peace of mind can come to a person who lives by the Words of our Lord.

44

Expression: Gave up the ghost

Location: Genesis 25:8

Verse: Then Abraham gave up the ghost [breathed his last], and died in a good old age, an old man, and full of years; and was gathered to his people [joined his deceased relatives in death].

The sergeant sternly stood beside his group of army recruits as he gave instructions before sending this fearful group of new recruits through the obstacle course training.

An obstacle course is made up of barriers which require some physical strength and agility. For instance, a recruit may be expected to jump a series of obstructions, climb up a rope ladder, swing on bars across a pond, crawl under various impediments, and pull up over a high wall by using only a rope.

It was this last obstacle that caused a recruit some trouble. This one timid recruit had forgotten the sergeant's instructions. The sergeant insisted that to get over the wall, one must grasp the rope up high, thereby giving strength to the body. This recruit held the rope down low and found it impossible to pull the whole weight of his body over the wall.

After many attempts and many failures, the recruit had to give up on that obstacle and walk around the wall in defeat. This is a time when we might say, "He gave up the ghost!"

We use this expression meaning anything from simply giving up on an attempt to literally dying. In the Bible this expression means that the person died.

The New Testament presents this expression a number of times. The Gospels speak of Jesus on the cross: "And when Jesus had cried with a loud voice, he said, 'Father, into thy hands I commend my spirit'; and having said thus, he gave up the ghost" (Luke 23:46).

45

Expression: **Get behind me, Satan**

Location: Luke 4:8

Verse: And Jesus answered and said unto him, Get thee behind me, Satan: for it is written, Thou shalt worship the Lord thy God, and him only shalt thou serve.

This expression is known by all to have a religious context. This would indicate that every person is within the reach of goodness. When people say, "Get behind me, Satan," they are admitting two things: they are admitting that evil is wrong, and they are admitting that they should resist it.

Jesus lived a sinless life. He actually spoke these words on two different occasions according to the Bible.

The scripture tells of Jesus saying this when he was tempted by the devil during his forty days in the wilderness. As Jesus was tempted, it affected the body, the soul, and the spirit.

In the verse above from the book of Luke, Jesus is referring to where it is written in the Old Testament scripture, in Deuteronomy 6:13.

Jesus Christ was tempted, and he denied temptation to demonstrate that you and I have a sinless Savior.

Satanic temptation is present in our lives today. All of us need the expression, "Get behind me, Satan."

46

Expression: Gird up your loins

Location: 1 Peter 1:13

Verse: Wherefore gird up the loins of your mind, be sober, and hope to the end for the grace that is to be brought unto you at the revelation of Jesus Christ.

The football coach in the height of a pressured moment yelled, "Gird up your loins and block!"

In biblical times, men wore loose, flowing garments around their hips and lower abdomen. To gird up one's loins meant to tuck the knee-length, shirtlike tunic under one's belt.

Most of the time this expression probably implies encountering some objective that requires some physical strength. The expression can also be a figure of speech in referring to a person's mental attitude in achieving. This is the way that Bible verse above is used.

Peter, in writing this epistle [letter] to Jewish believers around A.D. 65, was asking them to separate themselves from sin. Peter stressed that holiness of life involves mental alertness.

This verse of scripture implies for one to be mentally alert, prepare one's mind for action, to discipline oneself, be serious, and have hope.

47

Expression: Go the second mile

Location: Matthew 5:41

Verse: And whosoever shall compel thee to go a mile, go with
him [that person] twain [the second mile].

In our present culture, to "go the second mile" is to do more
than is expected or required of us — to go beyond the call of duty.
Many "go the second mile" in their workplace, serving others and
giving of themselves.

Dr. H.C. Morrison was considered by many to be one of the
greatest evangelical orators during the first part of the twentieth
century. He was the president of Asbury College in Wilmore, Ken-
tucky. Dr. Morrison asked God many times for guidance with the
problems of building the college. But he didn't stop there. He was
known to pray so hard and intensely that he would pray himself to
his knees on the floor in his office. Dr. Morrison always went the
second mile.

However, to "go the second mile" in the verse above has a
slightly different meaning through the teachings of Jesus. Jesus
teaches that it is more important to give justice and mercy than to
receive it, or retaliate against enemies. Jesus is counseling against
vindictiveness. He urges people to "turn the other cheek." Jesus
teaches us to "go the second mile."

48

Expression: God is my witness

Location: Romans 1:9

Verse: For [as] God is my witness, whom I serve with my spirit in the gospel of his Son, that without ceasing I make mention of you always in my prayers.

The movie reached an important climax when the actress shouted, "As God is my witness, I won't rest until I find my son."

In real life, two ladies were heard talking at the corner drugstore while standing in front of the cashier checkout counter. One was heard saying, "I am telling you the truth, as God is my witness."

To a tiny sect of Christian believers who were rising in Rome around 56 A.D., the apostle Paul wrote the longest of his thirteen New Testament letters. The book of Romans in the Bible speaks these words through Paul. He desires to visit the believers in Rome and writes the above proclaiming his love for them and for their Lord.

49

Expression: God is testing us

Location: Psalm 66:10

Verse: For thou, O God, hast proved [tested] us: thou hast tried [refined] us, as silver is tried.

A child of age seven can be deeply hurt by fellow playmates. I ran home crying on the day that my two friends plotted against me and said hard things. The real tragic event occurred when the two friends revealed that one of their families was going to take them to a basketball game, but I was not included. I thought that my heart would break. I ran home. My mother stopped what she was doing and shared the deep hurt that I was feeling.

My saintly mother comforted me and said, "God is testing you." God does indeed test us as the Psalmist wrote.

Just as one would refine metal to get out the impurities, times of distress offer a testing of God's people as to their trust and loyalty. Trials can refine one's character.

James, who is considered by many to be the half-brother of Jesus and a leader in the Jerusalem church, has some very inspirational things to say in his writing. For instance: "Knowing this, that the trying [testing] of your faith worketh patience [perseverance]" (James 1:3).

50

Expression: God loves a cheerful giver

Location: 2 Corinthians 9:7

Verse: Every man [person] according as he [or she] purposeth [decides] in his [one's] heart, so let him [or her] give; not grudgingly [reluctantly], or of necessity [under compulsion]; for God loveth [loves] a cheerful giver.

The restaurant was noisy. A group of men which met for lunch that day had to speak rather loudly to be heard around the table. From a variety of topics, the conversation drifted to a discussion about giving to charities. You can imagine the diverse comments on this subject coming from this collection of individuals.

One man said irritably, "About ninety percent of all the mail we get at home is junk mail and people asking for money."

Another man said, "I'm not going to give a dime to anyone unless I can take it off my income tax."

A third person contributed to the tone of the discussion by saying, "My church asks for money as much as anybody."

One of the men, who was a leader in his church, said, "I feel that I have to give to my church because they expect it of me."

One member of the group who had been listening spoke up and said, "But, remember, God loves a cheerful giver."

God asks us to give cheerfully with love. God is concerned about how we give from the resources we have. It may mean that we give ten percent of all we have, or it may mean that we give much more than that. To be truthful, Jesus asks us to give everything to the Lord. Everything we have, possess, do, and think should be dedicated to noble uses for God and his work on this earth.

In Second Corinthians, the scripture emphasizes the abundant blessings from God to those who give. The scripture states that whoever gives little, will get little. If a farmer plants little, he will realize only a small crop. If the farmer plants much, he will reap much (2 Corinthians 9:6).

All blessings may not necessarily be material, but being blessed in a spiritual way is indeed an exhilarating, soul-stirring experience of great joy.

If we give grudgingly or for recognition, the gift loses its value.

If we give out of gratitude, generosity, and desire to help others, we will be blessed.

Those who receive our gifts will be helped, and they will see God's work in action.

God loves a cheerful giver.

51

Expression: God save the king

Location: 1 Samuel 10:24

Verse: And Samuel said to all the people, See ye him whom the
Lord hath chosen, that there is none like him among all the
people? And all the people shouted, and said, God save the
king.

If asked where this expression has been heard, some people
probably would say boastfully, "Why that originated in the great
epic movies." Many people might say that it was an expression
from old English days when people shouted, "God save the king."
True, the expression has been present from England to Hollywood. We also find this expression in the Bible.
When the Israelites, the chosen people of God, had wandered
and continued to reject and disobey their God, they first thought
that having judges over the people would be their answer. Then
they changed and decided they wanted a king over their nation. So
Samuel, the last of the judges and considered the first of the prophets, brought all of the tribes of Israel together and presented to
them Saul, who was to be their king. And the people shouted, "God
save the king!"

52

Expression: God works in mysterious ways

Location: Ephesians 3:9

Verse: And to make all men [people] see what is the fellowship [plan] of the mystery [divine secret], which from the beginning of the world [ages] hath been hid [hidden] in God, who created all things....

How many times have we heard this expression used? The actual expression, "God works in mysterious ways," does not appear in the Bible. However, there are many references in the Bible to the mysterious, and it is possible that people developed this expression from the mere fact that the Bible does explain that God's mysterious ways are true. This truth is revealed in the verse above.

We may say that "mystery" is a truth, a divine secret and purpose of God known only by divine revelation. The apostle Paul writes much about receiving revelations of the mysteries. God's "mystery" is a plan that God is actively working out and revealing stage by stage. Every believer is a receiver of the mysterious. We today are "stewards of the mysteries of God" (1 Corinthians 4:1). We are to spread this message of God to others.

53

Expression: Going to the dogs

Location: Matthew 15:26

Verse: ... It is not meet [fair] to take the children's bread, and to cast [throw] it to dogs.

It is almost impossible to listen to a speech by a politician, educator, or religious leader without hearing them somewhere along the way declare that our country, our youth, and our morals are going to the dogs.

I recall one of my college professors reading a lengthy essay to our class which vividly expressed how the present culture was leading the people to condemnation and damnation, and was rapidly going to the dogs. When he finished the essay, he gave the name of the philosopher, who lived and wrote during the sixteenth century.

There is a story in the book of Matthew concerning the faith of a Canaanite woman, a Gentile. This Canaanite woman came crying to Jesus to have mercy on her. She told him that her daughter was terribly sick. The woman came and knelt before Jesus and asked for his mercy. When the woman pleaded for his help, Jesus replied with the words in the verse above.

Jesus certainly was not degrading the woman by using this term. Jesus possibly was reflecting the people's attitude so as to contrast it with his own.

In the next verse the woman says, "... yet the dogs eat of the crumbs which fall from their masters' table" (Matthew 15:27). The woman was willing to settle for crumbs to get help for her daughter.

Then Jesus answered and said, "O woman, great is thy faith: be it [done] unto thee even as thou wilt [wish]." And the woman's daughter was made well from that very hour (Matthew 15:28).

Jesus can lift our burdens. Jesus came to save all people of faith.

54

Expression: The Golden Rule

Location: Matthew 7:12

Verse: ... Whatsoever ye would that men [others] should do to you, do ye even so to them....

Many people know the Golden Rule, and many people at times use it as a reference; but, oh, how they often get so tangled in the wording.

A local radio station employed a device of the "old radio days" by having a "man on the street" broadcast. The radio announcer with a microphone went out into the downtown section of the city, stood on a busy street corner, and asked people as they passed by, "Can you tell me what the Golden Rule is?"

Many eyes brightened as people felt that they knew the answer. But here are some of their exact words:

"Do to others what you want them to do to you."

"Don't do anything to somebody that you don't want done to you."

"Do good to others and they will do good to you."

"Don't treat other people like you would not want them to treat you."

In the Bible, Jesus makes this teaching more significant by stating it in a positive way, rather than saying not to do something to someone.

From the book of Matthew in the King James Version of the Bible, the exact wording is: "... Whatsoever ye would that men [others] should do to you, do ye even so to them...."

55

Expression: A good name is better than great riches

Location: Proverbs 22:1

Verse: A good name is rather to be chosen than great riches, and
loving favor [esteem] rather than silver and gold.

I committed a criminal act when I was ten years old. Immediately I felt guilty. My conscience began to hurt me. When I arrived back home, my pain forced me to tell my mother.

I explained to my mother that when I went to the grocery store for her, I passed by the large open barrel of peanuts. I reached over, took a peanut out of the barrel, and ate it. I was a thief.

My mother explained that it would be easier and easier to commit wrong as I got used to it. She explained that if I could steal a peanut, it could then be easy to pick up an apple. If I could do that, then putting an apple in each pocket would seem easy. My actions could move on from one act to a larger act.

Then my mother looked me in the eyes and said, "A good name is better than great riches." That made me want to possess "a good name."

Many of us grew up in a poor family during the Great Depression of the 1930s — poor with regard to money and material possessions. But we can be proud that we grew up with character and a good name. That is something that we can always count as our riches.

56

Expression: The good old days

Location: Ecclesiastes 7:10

Verse: Say not thou [do not say], What is the cause that the former [good old] days were better than these? For thou [you] dost [do] not inquire wisely [out of wisdom] concerning this.

Old-timers like this writer can always find a reason to refer to the good old days. But one doesn't have to be very old to speak of the good old days.

When I speak of the good old days, I usually refer to the Golden Age of Radio, the concert in the park, the circus putting up its huge tent, or our family riding the streetcar to town to go shopping. However, recently I heard a college-age student refer to the good old days. He was reminiscing about the times he and his family went out to the lake, had a picnic on the ground, and then went fishing.

When we think about the good old days, our minds seem to have a way of filtering out the bad experiences and problems that I am sure we were having back during those good old days. But the pleasantness of those times brings sweet memories to our lives.

The Bible also speaks about the good old days. The Living Bible paraphrases Ecclesiastes 7:10 by using these words:

"Don't long for the good old days, for you don't know whether they were any better than these!"

57

Expression: The handwriting on the wall

Location: Daniel 5:7 (TLB)

Verse: ... Whoever reads that [hand] writing on the wall, and tells me what it means, will be dressed in purple robes of royal honor with a gold chain around his neck, and become the third ruler in the kingdom!

About fifty miles south of present-day Baghdad, Iraq, lie the ruins of the ancient city of Babylon.

It was October 12 in the year 539 B.C. when Belshazzar, the ruling regent of Babylon, was in a partying mood. At that very moment a warring enemy was literally at his gate, but Belshazzar was unconcerned. He wanted to have a big party at the palace.

Belshazzar apparently couldn't imagine his enemy overtaking his well-fortified city. Secular history tells us that the city wall was fifteen miles square and was constructed of brick. It was 300 feet high and wide enough for four chariots to travel abreast around the city walls. Today we would call that a freeway or an interstate.

In the Bible, Daniel describes this partying night of horror. Belshazzar invited hundreds of his officers and their guests to a great feast where the wine flowed freely. While Belshazzar was drinking, he was reminded of the gold and silver cups which had been taken long before from the Temple in Jerusalem during the reign of Nebuchadnezzar.

When Nebuchadnezzar took Jerusalem, he was a pagan and heathen king, and he delighted in taking the sacred vessels, from the Temple. But when he came to believe in God, he had the vessels stored away.

Belshazzar remembered these sacred cups, and he ordered that they be brought in to the feast. When they arrived, he and his guests drank toasts from these cups to their idols of gold, silver, brass, iron, wood, and stone (Daniel 5:4). These very vessels that they were profaning were once dedicated to God by King Solomon.

Suddenly, as the people were drinking from these cups, they saw the fingers of a human hand writing on the wall. Belshazzar saw it and was struck with fear. In his terror Belshazzar screamed out for his magicians to come to him. He then frantically instructed them to read and explain the writing.

Later the queen-mother told him about a man named Daniel who worshiped God and could help him. Belshazzar immediately sent for Daniel. When Daniel came and stood in the throne room, Belshazzar asked him if he was the same man that his grandfather, King Nebuchadnezzar, had brought from Israel as a Jewish captive. Belshazzar said that he understood Daniel served God, was filled with enlightenment and wisdom, and could solve all kinds of mysteries. Belshazzar offered Daniel the same rewards as he had his magicians, including making him the third ruler in the kingdom.

Why the third ruler? Belshazzar was never technically the king of Babylon, though he was called that. His father, Nabonidus, was still living and Belshazzar was really only a regent. This explains why he could offer only the third place in the kingdom.

Daniel refused his gifts, but he told Belshazzar what the handwriting on the wall meant. First, Daniel told this sinful ruler that he had defied the Lord of Heaven when he brought in the sacred cups from the Temple, and that his officers, wives, and concubines had been drinking wine from these holy cups while praising other meaningless gods and idols. Daniel told Belshazzar that he failed to praise the God who gave him breath and life and who controlled his destiny. Daniel told him that God had sent those fingers to write the message on the wall. The message said that God had numbered the days of his reign. God had weighed him in his scales, and he had failed the test. Daniel said that the kingdom would be divided and given to the Medes and Persians.

Even at this, Belshazzar probably laughed and decided to return to his attitude of "eat, drink, and be merry.'

Needless to say, the enemy entered the city. Babylon fell like water over a cliff. The scripture states that on that night, Belshazzar, the king of the Chaldeans, was killed (Daniel 5:30). Belshazzar had ignored the handwriting on the wall.

58

Expression: Heap coals of fire on one's head

Location: Romans 12:20

Verse: Therefore if thine enemy hunger, feed him [or her]; if he [she] thirst, give him [her] drink: for in so doing thou [you] shalt [will] heap coals of fire on his [or her] head.

Children can be very cruel. For a child's peer to say something hurtful can cause more heartaches and anguish than being disciplined by an adult.

All of us have experienced this kind of hurt many times as children. We need a loving mother or father to whom we can go and express our true feelings.

The wise and loving parent told the child not to try to get even. The parent said, "Heap coals of fire on their heads." Then the parent began to explain and discuss the matter more fully.

The parent said that this expression has to do with offering understanding to everyone, including our enemies. By being kind to our enemies, and thereby heaping coals of fire on them, they will feel ashamed of themselves for what they have done to us. And our actions might bring them closer to God.

59

Expression: Holier than thou

Location: Isaiah 65:3, 5

Verse: A people that provoketh me to anger continually ... Which say, Stand by thyself, come not near to me; for I am holier than thou....

No one likes a smart aleck. No, that expression is not in the Bible. But "holier than thou" is!

A smart aleck is conceited and feels superior to others. He is impudent, an egotist, a swaggerer. Yes, this too defines a "holier than thou" smart aleck.

Isaiah attached this expression to the people committing all kinds of sins. Those who engaged in pagan rituals believed that they were superior to others. They falsely believed that they were "holier than thou."

60

Expression: How long, oh, how long!

Location: Exodus 10:3

Verse: Thus saith the Lord God of the Hebrews, How long wilt thou refuse to humble thyself before me? Let my people go, that they may serve me.

Is this expression used all over the country? Or is it just a Tennessee expression? Let me explain.

It was the summer of 1948 — July, to be exact. Television sets were still an oddity in the home. Those who owned a set always invited others in to watch.

The summer of 1948 was not only exciting because we could watch this new invention which brought real, live, pictorial events into our home, but this particular summer also brought the very educational exposure of the two national political party conventions into our living room via the television screen.

We Tennesseans had great interest in watching the Democratic convention from Philadelphia. The keynote speaker for the convention was Frank Clement — Governor Frank Clement of Tennessee.

Politician Frank Clement was admired regardless of one's political preference. He was a family man and a church man. He taught a Sunday school class at a local Methodist church in Nashville.

On this summer night in 1948, everyone was watching the keynote speaker with great interest. Once in a while the television camera would focus on President Harry Truman. Mr. Truman could be seen smiling at his wife Bess in a very pleasant way as he was approving of the words coming from the charismatic and dynamic keynote speaker.

An expression that many people and newspapers picked up on and remembered from the speech by Governor Clement was the phrase, "How long, oh, how long," as Governor Clement drew out the word "oh" in his southern drawl.

This expression is from the Bible. Of course, Governor Clement knew it was from the Bible and used it very effectively as he promoted his party's views and platform.

In the Old Testament, Moses and Aaron came into the presence of Pharaoh and said in effect, "How long, oh, how long?"

61

Expression: A hypocrite

Location: Matthew 23:27

Verse: Woe unto you ... hypocrites! For ye are like unto [just like] whited [whitewashed] sepulchres [tombs], which indeed appear beautiful outward, but are within [inside] full of dead men's [people's] bones, and of all uncleanness.

In school what did you learn as the definition of the word "hypocrite"? Simply said, a hypocrite is one who affects virtues or qualities he or she does not have.

Mel and Hank were coworkers. Mel felt that Hank needed a better relationship with God, to state it in a tactful way. Mel didn't attempt to preach to Hank, but he often dropped a phrase or two his way, hoping to shed a little light on the matter concerning a relationship with God. Mel hoped that the personal witness of his own life would say something to Hank without always having to use words.

One day Mel was rather shocked when Hank said, "Why don't you go to church with me next Sunday?"

Mel had no indication at all that Hank ever went to church. Mel smiled and quickly answered, "I certainly will." Mel saw this move as a way he might get a little closer to witnessing to Hank.

The next Sunday morning the two met and drove to Hank's church together. Mel had never been in this particular church and was very much looking forward to attending the service there.

They came to the church, parked the car, and went inside. Hank told Mel where he could sit. Hank said, "I'll be back later and we'll sit together when the worship service starts."

Mel took his seat, began to read the church bulletin for the worship service, and in a moment looked up to see Hank playing an entirely different role from what Mel had seen before.

This fellow, Hank, had placed a white carnation in his coat lapel, had a handful of bulletins, and was greeting people at the door. He was all smiles and saying proper things to the congregational members as they entered the door.

This was definitely not the person with whom Mel worked daily! During the week, Hank never showed any love or compassion for his fellow workers. During a normal week, Hank certainly displayed his greed, self-indulgence, selfishness, and crookedness in business dealings.

On this particular Sunday morning, this gentleman put on an excellent act with his piety, pomp, and splendor. He was what Henry H. Halley called an "irreligious professional religionist."

Mel sat there in the church pew completely stunned. Mel thought to himself, "What an actor. What a hypocrite."

The word "hypocrisy" actually comes from the Greek word *hypokrisis,* which means the act of playing a part on the stage. A hypocrite is an actor.

Hypocrites are referred to in the Bible in Job, Psalms, Proverbs, and Isaiah in the Old Testament and in Matthew, Mark, and Luke in the New Testament.

In Matthew 23:27, we find Jesus speaking to the multitudes and to his disciples about hypocrites. This simile of the whitewashed tomb may be a picture of many churchgoers today — they are beautiful on the outside, but on the inside they are dead in trespasses and sins. They are not new creatures in Christ. They are merely good actors — hypocrites.

62

Expression: If you don't work, you don't eat

Location: 2 Thessalonians 3:10

Verse: ... if any would not work, neither should he [anyone be
allowed to] eat.

A pastor was counseling a young father and his son who had
dropped by his study one day. Both the father and son apparently
were under great stress and in a very emotional state. The pastor
felt great compassion for both of them as they seemed so distressed
that they could not communicate with calmness.

The father shouted at his son, "You are out of school now. You
are not going to just sit around and have your hoodlum friends
over and never do any work. From now on, if you don't work, you
don't eat!"

There was a great separation between this father and son because of their approach to each other. The father simply angered
his son by shouting orders at him and talking to him as one less
than a human being. His approach should have been a true desire
to discuss and understand his son's feelings. In fact, God says,
"Come, let us reason together" (Isaiah 1:18).

The son should not have slumped in the chair, mumbled under
his breath, and showed fierce anger in the expression on his face
with his jaw set, implying that he would never cooperate.

The pastor's counseling and remarks to both these friends that
day did some good. The pastor helped them to be able to communicate better and show more respect for each other.

Of course, there is some scriptural truth in what the father
shouted that day.

Second Thessalonians is the second of Paul's letters which was
written around 51 A.D. from Corinth to the Christians in Thessalonica, Greece.

Possibly due to their location on a famous highway from Rome to the east, the Thessalonians were exposed to false teachers who tried to tell them that the second coming of Christ was very close at hand. Therefore, many people left their jobs to sit and wait for the Lord's return.

In this letter Paul scolds the able-bodied for their laziness and for not working. Paul speaks against loafing and taking handouts. He wants them to work for a living — to make the most of their talent and time. Paul reminds them that when he was there with them on a visit, he gave them the principle that "if you don't work, you don't eat."

63

Expression: In due season

Location: Galatians 6:9

Verse: And let us not be weary in well-doing; for in due season we shall reap, if we faint not [do not give up].

Good will come to believers in due season. This is a promise from God.

One of the greatest examples of a person who reaped in due season what she had sown was Jochebed, the mother of Moses. Because of the terrible times in which she lived, and the possibility of her child's being killed, she devised a plan to save the life of her son, Moses. She placed him a reed basket and set him out on the river. He was found and adopted by Pharaoh's daughter. Moses was to grow up in the splendor of the palace in Egypt.

By God's wonderful arrangement, Jochebed was the one to be his nursemaid in the palace. She taught Moses about God and his Jewish religion, which included the knowledge of Abraham and God's purpose for Israel.

Jochebed saw her son grow into a man. She never gave up when all Egypt was against her beliefs. Her son grew up as an Egyptian, with their culture, their philosophy, and their sinful pleasures. But patience and time saw Moses forsake the pleasures and sins of Egypt, and Moses went on to be a great leader for his God.

64

Expression: In the twinkling of an eye

Location: 1 Corinthians 15:52

Verse: In a moment, in the twinkling of an eye, at the last trump:
for the trumpet shall sound, and the dead shall be raised
incorruptible [imperishable], and we shall be changed.

Carolyn and Tom were invited to their pastor's home for dinner. The pastor and his wife wanted to show appreciation for the
many volunteer jobs they had done at the church, especially regarding the music program.

Both Tom and Carolyn are very outgoing, enthusiastic, spirited
people with a great sense of humor. People found it always a happy
experience to be in their company.

On this particular evening, the doorbell rang, and the pastor
briskly headed for the door. Carolyn and Tom hurried inside in the
most rushed and hyperactive manner one could imagine. Immediately, Tom began to speak in a very excited way. He said, "You
don't know when it is going to happen. It can happen when you
least expect it. It happened in the twinkling of an eye."

Carolyn and Tom had had a minor auto accident — a fender-
bender — on their way to the house. The pastor quickly inquired if
anyone had been hurt. Luckily, no.

Then he understood the frenzied words of Tom. Yes, a car wreck
usually happens in the twinkling of an eye. In the fifteenth chapter
of First Corinthians (Paul's first letter to the people of the church
in Corinth, Greece), Paul is strenuously trying to convince the
people there to choose eternal life. Paul explained that there are
first human bodies, and then later spiritual and heavenly bodies on
our resurrection.

The scripture states that this change will take place in a split
second — in a moment — in the twinkling of an eye. The phrase is
en atomo, which defines a very small particle of time. We get our
word "atom" from this Greek word.

85

65

Expression: Inherit the wind

Location: Proverbs 11:29

Verse: He [one] that troubleth [unsettles] his [one's] own house [family] shall inherit the wind [evil]; and the fool shall be servant to the wise of heart.

Playwrights Jerome Lawrence and Robert Lee were certainly cognizant of the biblical text when they gave their play the title, *Inherit the Wind*. The playwrights depicted the courtroom battle over the constitutionality of teaching the opinion of evolution in the schools, based on Clarence Darrow and William Jennings Bryan in the famous Tennessee Scopes trial.

This verse from Proverbs deals with the great resources of the family. Good families provide encouragement and guidance. The word "wind" in this biblical expression may be taken as a metaphor for evil. Those who cause trouble within their families can expect to inherit evil.

66

Expression: It is more blessed to give than to receive

Location: Acts 20:35

Verse: It is more blessed to give than to receive.

I can pinpoint the day I first heard this beautiful expression. It was Christmas Day when I was nine years old.

Christmas Day, when my sister and I were young, was a pause in history — a time when all hardships and sorrow were not felt or even thought of. Christmas Day included a special breakfast that my mother prepared. Our father turned on the lights to our live tree which we had decorated the night before. After our family had shared our gifts, my sister and I started out in the fresh, crisp air of winter to the homes in the neighborhood. We were excited to see what everyone got for Christmas. We carried in a basket the gifts we were going to give to various friends along the way.

I shall never forget one family that had recently moved into the neighborhood. There was a nine-year-old boy in that family also. To show the spirit of being a good neighbor, my mother had helped me wrap a small gift so I could present it to this new boy.

My sister and I knocked on the door of this new family in the neighborhood. We were welcomed inside. We could tell immediately that the family was very poor. There were no signs of Christmas. I handed my present to the new boy. His face lit up.

Being a child of nine years, I thought they would find a gift to hand to me. My mother always had a few "spares" wrapped for emergencies such as this. But I received no gift. I did receive a "thank you"   that was more genuine than any I had ever received in the past.

My sister and I soon left their home and headed back to our house. I tried not to show any disappointment. I didn't even say a word to my sister as we walked back home, but when I arrived home, my mother could tell that something was wrong. In fact, she knew everything. When we finally began to talk about my not getting a gift from the new boy in the neighborhood, my mother patiently explained to me that it was more blessed to give than to receive. On Christmas Day when I was nine years old, I completely understood.

In thinking back to that new nine-year-old boy who had moved to my neighborhood, I realized that his happiness, joy, and feeling of being liked was far, far greater than any small gift he may have handed me on that Christmas Day.

67

Expression: Judge not, that you be not judged

Location: Matthew 7:1

Verse: Judge not, that ye be not judged.

On a beautiful, sunny summer day, two ladies were seated on a park bench as they watched the other people in the park. The ladies' eyes darted back and forth as they took in every single thing that happened among the other people.

The beauty of the day, the fragrance of the flowers, the smiles on people's faces, and the little children having a wonderful day in the park with their parents seemed to go unnoticed by the two ladies. Their attention was on how awful people looked, who should reduce, what they should not have worn, how they should fix their hair, and yes, the children made too much noise.

These two ladies on the park bench must have thought they were without faults. They had set themselves up as judges over everyone they saw. What a perfect situation for the expression, "Judge not, that you be not judged."

Jesus taught that this is a good philosophy by which to live. Jesus continues to speak in the next verse, which helps us to understand more: "For with what judgment ye judge, ye shall be judged: and with what measure ye mete [use], it shall be measured to you again" (Matthew 7:2).

68

Expression: Judgment day

Location: John 12:48

Verse: ... The word that I [Christ] have spoken, the same shall judge him [all] in the last day.

"That blessed soul shall receive her crown of jewels in heaven on judgment day" was spoken by the nephew looking at his beloved aunt lying on her deathbed.

"That dear woman will receive her reward on judgment day" was heard spoken by a friend who had been in awe for years of the compassion and self-giving of this saintly woman.

It is possible to hear the same type expression when it means the exact opposite. The person shouted, "That man will receive his just reward on judgment day!" The person was angry and totally disapproving of this man's action.

Judgment day seemed to be the first thing that entered the minds of these observers in approving or disapproving of a person. We have to be very thankful that the consequences of judgment day are not left up to a verdict by a human being or a jury of twelve. We are very thankful that we can trust a living God.

When the expression "judgment day" is used, we generally think of God's final judgment at the end of time and the beginning of eternity.

69

Expression: Keep the faith

Location: 2 Timothy 4:7

Verse: I have fought a good fight, I have finished my course [race], I have kept the faith.

The place is Rome. The time is about 66 A.D. Emperor Nero has imprisoned the apostle Paul in a horrible prison. Paul is chained like a common criminal. He is cold, and he asks Timothy to bring his cloak.

Paul knew that the day of his execution was nearing. This is when he wrote the Second Epistle [letter] to the young preacher, Timothy. In this letter Paul urged Timothy and his church to proclaim God's message, to be persistent, to encourage others, and to teach.

With Paul, there had been a battle to be fought and a victory to be won. Paul said that he had been faithful to his calling. Paul figuratively used the athlete running a race to describe his ministry.

Soon after writing this second letter to Timothy, the executioner's ax released Paul's soul to go and reside with God. Paul had kept the faith.

70

Expression: **Kill the fatted calf**

Location: Luke 15:22-23

Verse: ... the father said ... Bring forth the best robe ... and put a ring on his hand [finger], and shoes on his feet: And bring hither [here] the fatted calf, and kill it; and let us eat, and be merry [celebrate].

If a son or daughter comes home for a visit after being away for many months, the mother and father will rejoice and prepare a warm welcome.

The Bible tells of the prodigal son who finally returns home after much wandering. His father welcomes him with open arms and prepares a huge feast by killing the best calf he has.

All of the symbols in the scripture above were signs of position and acceptance. A long robe showed distinction, a signet ring showed authority, shoes or sandals were worn by a beloved child rather than going barefoot, and the "fatted calf" represented a very special occasion.

In ancient times there was the practice of separating some calves from their mothers and fattening them on special feed so as to develop fine calves for celebrations. This father in the story killed the fatted calf for his son. This father's love, just like God's, proved to be constant.

71

Expression: The kiss of death

Location: Mark 14:45

Verse: And as soon as he [Judas] was come [arrived], he [Judas] goeth straightway [immediately] to him [Jesus], and saith, Master, Master; and kissed him.

In the business world, when one partner wants to set forth a great amount of money on a speculative deal, and the other partner totally disagrees, that second partner might easily say, "I don't want to do it. That would be the kiss of death."

In a gangster movie we might see "a kiss of death," and we would know what that means.

The most important historical kiss of death was when Judas Iscariot accepted thirty pieces of silver to betray Jesus Christ in the Garden of Gethsemane some 2,000 years ago.

Judas agreed to identify Jesus for the Temple guards by going over to him and planting a kiss on Jesus' cheek. This made sure that the guards would arrest the right person. A kiss was not unusual as it was a token of respect with which disciples customarily greeted their rabbi. Judas gave Jesus "the kiss of death."

72

Expression: Land o' Goshen

Location: Genesis 46:28

Verse: And he sent Judah before him unto Joseph, to direct his face [way] unto Goshen; and they came into the land of Goshen.

I have very warm and beautiful memories of being a child and playing out in our backyard. Each day my mother would open the old screen door and call me in to eat my lunch. Maybe it was my mother's wonderful cooking that makes my memory of that experience pleasant.

Each day as I sat down at the table to eat lunch during the summertime with that beautiful warm sun streaming in around the trees, I also heard my mother listening to "Ma Perkins" on the radio. No one knew what television was back then. One could keep on working and have an ear tuned to the radio which brought much happiness, drama, music, and even a degree of serenity to one's life.

I can remember Ma Perkins along with Evey, Willie, Fay, and Shuffle. An expression that Ma Perkins would always use when she felt the need of an exclamation was "Land o' Goshen!" Based on the pure and beautiful life of "our own Ma Perkins" I am sure that she knew that was from the Bible.

The northeast section of the Nile delta region in Egypt nearest Palestine is usually termed "the land of Goshen." Here the Israelites under Jacob settled while Joseph was prime minister of Egypt (Genesis 46). The land was very fertile and was especially adapted to herds and flocks. Goshen was a valley some 35 miles long stretching from Lake Timsah to the Nile.

God had planned that Israel should be nurtured for a while in Egypt, which was the most advanced civilization of that day.

73

Expression: The land of milk and honey

Location: Deuteronomy 6:3

Verse: ... as the Lord God of thy fathers [ancestors] hath promised thee, in the land that floweth with milk and honey.

There are some good church school teachers, and there are some
not so good. For instance, children might hear about "the land of
milk and honey" in their church school classes for years. However, where it was, what it was, and how it relates to the Bible
never seem to be explained.

The new church school superintendent had the opportunity to
walk into a church school class of ten-year-olds. He was proud to
see the teacher standing before a large map making "the land of
milk and honey" really come alive. This teacher was showing the
class a present-day map where the students could become oriented
as to the placement of Israel and surrounding territory and coun-
tries. The students seemed very interested in how the Jordan River
flowed down into the Dead Sea. All of this made sense to them.

Then their teacher showed some excellent maps located in the
back of her Bible which took the students back to the time of the
Israelites being led by Moses to their eventual destination in "the
land of milk and honey." This is another name for "the Promised
Land" to which Moses led the Israelites for forty years out of their
bondage in Egypt.

The land which God promised to give to Israel, the descendants of Abraham, Isaac, and Jacob, was the land of Canaan — the
land of milk and honey.

74

Expression: **The last will be first, and the first will be last**

Location: Luke 13:30

Verse: And, behold, there are last which shall be first; and there are first which shall be last.

Two friends were standing in the checkout lane at the supermarket. Suddenly, a third person came up and jumped in line ahead of the two. One of the friends turned around toward the other and said from the corner of his mouth, "The last will be first, and the first will be last." That brought a smile. However, the scripture has more depth to it than that.

Actually, it is referring to the fact that all who answer the Lord's call to salvation and service can expect fairness in the reward received.

In Luke 13:30 the disciples ask Jesus the question of how many or few will be saved. In one of Jesus' parables, the "first" laborers who were hired thought that they should receive more wages than the "last" laborers who were hired, because the "first" laborers had worked more hours. Actually, the "first" laborers had been dealt with fairly, but they protested because others had been dealt with so generously.

The issue seems to be that those who are totally committed to serve the Lord will receive a reward based on faithfulness and not on the time or extent of service in the harvest season.

75

Expression: Let go and let God

Location: Proverbs 20:24

Verse: Man's [humanity's] goings [steps] are of the Lord; how can a man [person] then understand his [or her] own way?

They were the very best of friends in college. After several years passed, their meeting on the street was a pleasant surprise. One college chum had always been a very busy person. He was unique in devising ideas of how to make money. The passing of years had not changed him in this respect. The only change his friend, who was now a lawyer, could detect was his graying hair, some wrinkles in his face, and a more solemn and stern look on his face. He seemed to be very anxious and stressful.

The lawyer was a good sounding board for his friend, who began to talk and express his true feelings. He began to explain that anxiety and stress by saying, "I am having so many problems in my advertising business. I constantly have to try to stay a jump ahead of my competitors. Even within my own company, I have to ride herd on petty jealousies and people trying to stab me in the back. My wife is complaining that I am not at home enough. My children...."

He stopped his furious attack of words and then said, "I don't need to bother you with all this. I appreciate your talking with me, though. It has done me a lot of good. I've got to go."

Actually, the college friend had done all of the talking. His lawyer friend's listening was a big help. The lawyer did say one thing. Just as they were about to part, he put his arm around his friend's shoulder and said, "Why don't you let go and let God?" The other man looked at him with a smile and walked away.

It was about a week later that this good friend came by the lawyer's office. The gist of what he said to the lawyer as he relaxed in a chair was what a tremendous help he had been to him by what he had said the week before. He remarked, "Do you remember that you told me to let go and let God?"

"Yes, I believe in that expression."

"Well, that made a big impression on me. I thought about it. That day I went home and spent the evening with my family. I have begun reading my Bible again, and last Sunday all of us went to Sunday school and church."

He finished by saying, "I just wanted to drop by today and tell you."

The lawyer told him how happy he was and suggested getting together more often.

Inasmuch as the entire Bible is directed to teaching the Good News — God's plan for our salvation — then we might say that the premise of the whole Bible is, in fact, the expression "let go and let God." We should depend on God's plan for our decisions rather than our own faltering and struggling to handle everything on our own.

76

Expression: Let not your left hand know what your right hand does

Location: Matthew 6:3

Verse: But when thou doest [give] alms [a charitable deed], let not thy left hand know what thy right hand doeth [is doing].

The old gray-haired gentleman slowly moved up the stairway to the office of the high school principal. Arriving at the top of the stairs, he brushed his hair from his eyes and knocked on the door. The principal came to the door and welcomed him.

During their long conversation, the old gentleman stressed his interest in education and in the cultural development of the youth in the school. The old gentleman opened his timeworn wallet stuffed with papers and removed a check made out for one million dollars. It was a gift to this school.

Immediately, the principal jumped from his chair with many words of gratitude, exclaiming that he would call the newspaper. The old gentleman asked him not to. The principal in his enthusiasm said, "Well, let us hold a special assembly and have you as our guest." Again, the old gentleman requested that he not do that either.

After many ideas from the principal as to how they could show appreciation for the gift, the old gentleman finally put the idea to rest by giving the school principal a biblical answer as to why he wanted no publicity for giving the gift. The old gentleman simply said, "The Bible says to serve God in secret, and God who sees in secret will reward thee openly."

In this scripture as well as the verse quoted above, Jesus is teaching that one's motives for giving to God's work, whether it be money or serving others, must be pure. The motive must not be for one's own benefit or praise.

77

Expression: Like mother, like daughter

Location: Ezekiel 16:44 (TLB)

Verse: Like mother, like daughter — that is what everyone will say of you.

An aging man revealed the fact that he had lived his life never knowing his grandfathers. His father died when he was sixteen years old. He had experienced the pleasure of having a father-in-law, a brother-in-law, a wonderful son, and a son-in-law.

But it seems that his life had been greatly blessed mostly by women in the family. He had a dear grandmother, a loving mother, a caring big sister, the most incredible wife in the world, a beautiful daughter, and an adorable granddaughter. He was heard saying, "I thank God for the women in my life."

"Like mother, like daughter" in this man's life was a tremendous expression. For his daughter to be like his wife was truly an added blessing.

This expression is in the book of Ezekiel. But exactly what does it mean? The sixteenth chapter of the book of Ezekiel is an allegory about unfaithful Jerusalem at this particular time in history. In this chapter, the city of Jerusalem is personified, implying that it is a woman. The language reflects both God's and Ezekiel's disgust with Jerusalem's apostasy. The language is very graphic and vivid in portraying the sin and idolatry of Israel at this period of time. The "like mother, like daughter" expression refers to Jerusalem's continual and seemingly hereditary tendency toward sin and evil.

However, the chapter concludes in a most glorious way. God will keep his covenant with Israel. In spite of the sin of the people, their rebellion, their constant departure from God, and their backsliding, God will still keep his covenant.

God's Word says that eventually they will remember and be ashamed and know that he is God.

78

Expression: **Live by the sword, die by the sword**

Location: Matthew 26:52

Verse: ... Put up again [put away] thy sword into his [the sword's] place; for all they that take [live by] the sword shall perish with [by] the sword.

The Bible gives the account of Jesus' being arrested by the Temple guards. Simon Peter, one of Jesus' disciples, was standing near Jesus when the guards approached. Peter drew his sword and struck one of the men on the ear. Immediately, Jesus stopped Peter.

Peter was of the opinion that he should prevent what he saw as defeat. Peter didn't realize that Jesus had to die in order to have victory for us humans. Jesus complied with God's will. Jesus knew that God's kingdom would not be advanced with swords, but with faith and obedience.

79

Expression: The Lord giveth and the Lord taketh away

Location: Job 1:21

Verse: ... the Lord gave, and the Lord hath taken away; blessed [praised] be the name of the Lord.

Surely this expression has been used by many, but the words have been altered slightly to a more colloquial use.

The exact words in the King James Version of the Bible are: "The Lord gave, and the Lord hath taken away."

This expression was heard recently on a television game show. The studio audience was screaming at a young contestant to encourage him in his effort to answer his question before the time expired. He failed the task, but immediately his expression was, "Well, the Lord giveth and the Lord taketh away."

Job spoke similar words as these when he was being severely tested. Job's possessions and family members had been wiped out. But Job's faith led him to see the all-powerful hand of God at work, and that gave him calmness and peace even in the face of calamity.

80

Expression: Made light of it

Location: Matthew 22:5

Verse: But they made light of it, and went their ways.

Sometimes we are very zealous about a particular matter that has much importance in our lives. We can be hurt rather quickly when someone else "makes light of it."

Sometimes the news media "makes light of" something which we feel they shouldn't. There are some things in life that we probably should "make light of."

The verse above says that they paid no attention to it and went on. In this part of scripture, God is inviting humanity to accept him, obey him, and be able to enter his kingdom of heaven. As we know, all too many refuse God's invitation. We make light of it and go on our worldly way.

81

Expression: Many are called, but few are chosen

Location: Matthew 22:14

Verse: ... For many are called, but few are chosen.

In the Bible, Jesus presents a great amount of his teaching in parables. The word "parable" actually means "likeness." A parable gives a comparison of two objects for the purpose of teaching.

In Matthew 22 Jesus gives a parable to show that a marriage feast is like the Kingdom of Heaven. Jesus explains that the Kingdom of Heaven can be illustrated by the story of a king who prepared a great wedding dinner for his son. He invited many guests to the dinner. When the dinner was ready, the king sent messengers out to notify everyone that it was time to come. But the people refused to come. The king even sent out other servants to tell the people that everything was ready. It was time to come. Unfortunately the guests he had invited just laughed and went on about their worldly business.

Then the king directed his servants to go out into the street and invite everyone they saw. So they did. They brought back all they could find. Finally, the banquet hall was filled with guests.

Do you understand this parable? How this marriage feast is like the Kingdom of Heaven?

The king is God and his son is the Lord Jesus. The king sent forth his servants to the "lost sheep of the house of Israel." The servants were his apostles, and in the Old Testament the messengers were the prophets. But the Israelites rejected God's invitation. God sent others, but they refused to come. They even killed the messengers.

The king's saying "everything is ready" is hinting at the death of Christ on the cross and his salvation for believers. Then the king told his servants to go out into the streets and invite people in. This is the worldwide offer to salvation. It refers to the present age in which we live. All of us are invited.

Many have the invitation to salvation extended to them, but only a very few accept and are chosen.

82

Expression: The meek shall inherit the earth

Location: Psalm 37:11

Verse: But the meek shall inherit the earth; and shall delight themselves in the abundance of peace.

This expression is in both the Old and the New Testaments.

In Psalm 37, David contrasts the righteous and the wicked. He is saying that the wicked will certainly be judged, but the righteous who have been wronged should not be discouraged. The righteous who humble themselves before the Lord will be blessed.

In the New Testament, Jesus states as one of the Beatitudes, "Blessed are the meek: for they shall inherit the earth" (Matthew 5:5).

Jesus is teaching that the righteous need to look toward the blessings of Heaven. He teaches that the humble, the meek, the gentle-spirited will inherit the blessings of the Kingdom of God.

With humble attitudes, we should display no arrogance toward our fellow human beings.

83

Expression: **A merry heart is good medicine**

Location: Proverbs 17:22

Verse: A merry heart doeth good like a medicine: but a broken [downcast] spirit drieth the bones [makes one sick].

Our mind and emotions can affect our health and happiness. There is some excellent medical and psychological research from leading universities that does indeed link health and happiness.

A good mental attitude can better enable us to resist stress and ward off disease. The immune system can be less likely to break down. The brain can be awash with natural pain-relieving chemicals. Many people who have fallen ill have been known to alter dramatically the course of their illness. Our mental attitudes can influence our health in mysterious ways.

We need to maximize our potential to live more fulfilling lives. We must focus our mental energy toward rewarding productivity. We need our attitudes to reflect willpower and motivation. And especially we need to exercise hope and love.

This new field of endeavor is known by the two-dollar word "psychoneuroimmunology." The Bible didn't need this lengthy word to convey this thought. The same thing was stated in the Bible thousands of years ago as you see in Proverbs 17:22.

We can greet others with happiness; give a word of encouragement; have enthusiasm in whatever task we undertake; and have a positive outlook on the future.

We can be good medicine to others as well as to ourselves.

84

Expression: A millstone around one's neck

Location: Mark 9:42

Verse: And whosoever shall offend [cause to stumble] one of these little ones that believe in me [to lose faith], it is better for him [that person] that a millstone were hanged about his [that person's] neck, and he [that person] were cast into the sea.

The well-known professional athlete was looked up to by many young people as their great hero. True, the athlete was an outstanding ballplayer who exemplified the greatest skills in playing the game. But the wrongful, immoral teaching he gave the young people through his life's example damaged their thinking and actions. Role models have an opportunity to set a good example.

These young people who were led astray might say when finding themselves in darkness and in the bottomless pit, "I feel as though a millstone is around my neck." It certainly can be said about the one who caused those to stumble. This expression is in the Bible.

A millstone during biblical times was a heavy stone slab which was turned by a donkey in grinding grain.

Jesus is teaching that no one should damage the faith of another by being a poor witness.

85

Expression: Money is the root of all evil

Location: 1 Timothy 6:10

Verse: For the love of money is the root of all [kinds of] evil:
which while some coveted after [were greedy about], they
have erred [turned away] from the faith, and pierced themselves through with many sorrows.

An elderly couple had lived on their block in the city for nearly
fifty years. They had been good neighbors.

One day a moving van rolled up at the house next door to this
couple. As time went by, these new neighbors renovated their large,
beautiful old house, put in tasteful landscaping, and built a new
garage where they could park their expensive car.

The other neighbors on the block had not heard of any compli-
cations at all until one day at the barbershop, this well-established
old-timer next door to these new neighbors began to talk. He and
his wife were not happy.

It appeared that the complaints from this old couple were three-
fold. The new couple was originally from another part of the country — strike one! The new couple was young — strike two! But
strike three, the most damaging, was the fact that the couple was
extremely wealthy.

This old gentleman next door really showed his bias when he
blurted out, "And you know they are going to hell because money
is the root of all evil."

The old expression has been said and used, read and excused,
misled and abused. Read the exact Bible verse carefully.

Why do people say, "Money is the root of all evil," instead of
accurately reporting: "The love of money is the root of all evil"?
Some of these evils can be covetousness, greed, apostasy from the
faith, pain, and sorrow.

The evil is not in the wealth itself, but in the wrong attitude toward the wealth. Worldly wealth can certainly cause people to fall into many temptations that others never have to face. "Ungodly" wealth can prove to be a trap which snares and deprives one of freedom and life. People can be trapped into many foolish desires which may be so strong in their lives that these desires become irresistible and take the persons down to personal and moral ruin.

In the next verse, Paul is saying that we are to diligently pursue Christian virtues, such as righteousness, godliness, faith, love, patience, and gentleness (1 Timothy 6:11).

Money and wealth are not in themselves evil. But a love of this money and wealth can certainly cause a person great sorrow.

86

Expression: A multitude of sins

Location: James 5:20

Verse: Let him [anyone] know, that he [one] which converteth
[brings back] the sinner from the error of his [or her] way
shall save a soul from death, and shall hide [have forgiven]
a multitude of sins.

It was surprising to hear a little five-year-old playing with her
young playmate out in the sandbox exclaim, "Oh, yes, that will
cover a multitude of sins."

Obviously, she had heard her parent or some other adult use the
expression with regard to arriving at some decision that would help
overcome a number of problems.

If someone has lost faith in God, and another person helps the
backslider to return to trust in God, then that person has saved the
wandering soul's separation from God. The person has helped bring
about the forgiveness of the wanderer's multitude of sins.

87

Expression: My cup runneth over

Location: Psalm 23:5

Verse: Thou preparest a table before me in the presence of mine enemies: thou anointest my head with oil; my cup runneth over.

Psalm 23 is probably the most beautiful and popular Psalm of all.

In biblical Middle Eastern culture, when at a banquet, it was customary to anoint a person with fragrant oil as a lotion. Also, it can be symbolic of the Holy Spirit.

An overflowing cup is used as a symbol for a life of abundance and plenty. The psalmist is praising God. Psalm 23 is appropriate to be read at every Thanksgiving dinner.

88

Expression: **No honor in one's own country**

Location: John 4:44

Verse: For Jesus himself testified, that a prophet hath no honor in his own country.

A good musician returned to his home in Nashville after spending a few years out of the state. He is a very fine trumpet player, and was highly respected everywhere he played during the years he was away. In New York he played on recording sessions. While in California he played on recording dates, concerts, and played on the score of two movies.

The trumpeter said that returning home to Nashville, he seemed to have a great deal of trouble getting hired for television shows and recording dates. Everyone looked upon him as the local fellow who had been away for a few years. He seemed quite despondent as he looked up one day and said, "A person has no honor in his own country."

Jesus wisely stated this same expression with regard to himself. It is reported in each of the four gospels.

89

Expression: **No one can serve two masters**

Location: Matthew 6:24

Verse: No man [one] can serve two masters; for either he [or she] will hate the one, and love the other; or else he [or she] will hold [be loyal] to the one, and despise the other. Ye [you] cannot serve God and mammon.

Mammon is a Semitic word for money or riches. We cannot place God first in our lives if we really have our hearts in this world of material wealth and possessions rather than on the world to come. This world lasts only for a little while, whereas God's world to come lasts forever. Halley's *Bible Handbook* says it so well:

> *Christians are citizens of heaven, sojourners here a while, cumbered with daily earthly cares, but their eyes ever fixed on the eternal homeland. An estate there which we build here. Only that which we give to God is ours forever. Said one man to another, of an acquaintance who had just died, "How much did he leave?" Answered the other, "He left it all." Even so. Shortly we must, everyone of us, quit our earthly tent, and leave to others that which we called ours. Fortunate for us if we have sent on ahead for a reservation in the Eternal Mansions of God.*

All must make a choice. Jesus said that the one that is not with me is against me (Matthew 12:30). No one can serve two masters.

90

Expression: No place to lay one's head

Location: Matthew 8:20

Verse: ... The foxes have holes, and the birds of the air have nests, but the Son of Man hath not [no place] where to lay his head.

A speaker came to the college campus and was going to speak on "Was Jesus a homeless person?" This was an intriguing title. Jesus did make some statements with regard to having no home of his own and having no place to lay or rest his head.

When Jesus was on a preaching mission, one of the religious scribes came up to him. A scribe was like a lawyer who made a systematic study of the religious law and its exposition. This scribe told Jesus that he would follow him no matter where he went. Then Jesus spoke the words you see above.

Following Jesus is not always comfortable or the easy thing to do. However, the rewards of being Christ's disciple are extremely valuable. They last for eternity.

91

Expression: No room in the inn

Location: Luke 2:7

Verse: And she [Mary] brought forth her firstborn son, and wrapped him in swaddling clothes [bands of cloth], and laid him [Jesus] in a manger, because there was no room for them in the inn.

This popular expression can be heard from many people in varied situations. A man, after finding a "no vacancy" sign at the motel, looked at his wife and children and said, "No room in the inn."

Many churches of all denominations now have programs set up to help the homeless and needy by offering food, shelter, and counseling in helping them find jobs. It is understandable that the name of the program would be "Room in the Inn."

Back in the first century, Emperor Caesar Augustus decreed that a census should be taken throughout the whole Roman empire. The citizens had to return to their ancestral homes for this registration. Because Joseph was from Bethlehem, he and Mary had to travel there for the census taking. While they were there, the time came for Mary to give birth to her baby. It is interesting to note that Jesus' being born in Bethlehem was prophesied in the Old Testament book of Micah, which was written hundreds of years before the birth of Christ (Micah 5:2).

Mary and Joseph found no room in the inn. An excellent metaphor is the room in people's hearts for the poor and needy.

92

Expression: O death, where is thy sting?

Location: 1 Corinthians 15:54-55

Verse: So when this corruptible [perishable body] shall have put on incorruption [imperishability], and this mortal [body] shall have put on immortality, then shall be brought to pass the saying that is written, Death is swallowed up in victory. O death, where is thy sting [victory]?

This expression may not be on the lips of a huge number of people very often. However, a dear grandmother who had her sights on God's Kingdom, knowing that she would not be swallowed up by death, spoke this to her children from her deathbed.

In First Corinthians, the apostle Paul continues his discussion of the believers' human bodies becoming heavenly, spiritual bodies when they are resurrected to go and be with the Lord.

When this change takes place "in the twinkling of an eye," then the scripture of the prophets Isaiah and Hosea in the Old Testament comes true. God will swallow up death in victory (Isaiah 25:8). God will redeem us from death (Hosea 13:14). God is going to win. Love will triumph. God is in control.

93

Expression: O ye of little faith

Location: Matthew 6:30

Verse: Wherefore, if God so clothe the grass of the field, which today is [alive] and tomorrow is cast [thrown] into the oven [fire], shall he not much more clothe you, O ye of little faith?

In Chattanooga, Tennessee, the citizens will proudly show you their Lookout Mountain Incline Railway, which is one of the steepest incline railways in the world. In fact, at its highest point, the gradient reaches 72.7 percent. The railway car starts from St. Elmo Avenue in Chattanooga and goes right up the side of Lookout Mountain. This ride reveals a spectacular view and is a very enjoyable trip.

An elderly man who served as the conductor aboard the railway car was an added attraction. He was very pleasant and humorous. When the car was filled with passengers and began its movement up the mountain, this man would begin to have fun, especially with the tourists. He would say scary things such as, "I wonder what would happen if the electric power went off." People would begin to squirm, and he would grin and say, "O ye of little faith."

As the car traveled on up to a great height and entered a portion of the track where it seemed that the car was tilted straight up, this old conductor would say, "I hope the cable doesn't break." Of course, the incline is safer than driving your car to the grocery store. But the people would moan and squirm, and the conductor would grin and say, "O ye of little faith."

This expression is found many times in the Bible. Matthew records these words of Jesus in chapter 6 verse 30.

94

Expression: Offers an olive branch

Location: Genesis 8:11

Verse: And the dove came in [back] to him [Noah] in the evening, and, lo, in her mouth [beak] was an olive leaf [branch] plucked off: so Noah knew that the waters were abated [receded] from off the earth.

During the Persian Gulf crisis in 1990-1991, a headline on the morning newspaper read: "President Bush Offers Olive Branch."

The general public understood the meaning of this expression. Offering an olive branch was symbolic of offering the peaceful environment in which things could be discussed and, hopefully, positive conclusions could be reached.

The modern symbol of peace which is often represented by a dove carrying an olive branch in its beak has its origin in the biblical account of Noah and the flood.

Noah, along with his family, were believers and had faith in God. They were saved from the flood which brought rain for forty days and forty nights. There was an enormous amount of water. In fact, the Bible refers to the deluge as coming from the fountains or springs of the great deep and the windows or floodgates of the heavens (Genesis 7:11).

The account of this flood reveals to us God's plan for salvation and judgment day. "Except ye repent, ye shall all likewise perish" (Luke 13:3). But the faith of Noah and his family depicts the saved of the world.

The waters flooded the earth for 150 days. But God remembered Noah; the word "remember" in the Bible is used to express great loving concern for someone and "with favor" (Nehemiah 5:19).

Finally, the great floods of water stopped, and the waters began to recede from the earth. On the seventeenth day of the seventh month, Noah's ark came to rest on the mountains of Ararat. The flood waters continued to recede until the tenth month. On the first day of the tenth month, Noah was able to see the tops of mountains which had become visible.

After forty days Noah opened the window in the ark and sent out a raven. The raven kept flying back and forth until the water had dried up from the earth. The raven never returned to the ark. Possibly the raven was able to eat the dead animals it found.

Then Noah sent out a dove to see if the water had receded from the surface of the ground. The dove could not find a resting spot on the surface of the earth, so it returned to Noah in the ark. Possibly the dove needed to find plant life to eat.

Noah waited seven more days and once again sent the dove out from the ark. That evening the dove returned to the ark with a freshly plucked olive leaf in its beak.

It is known that olives do not grow at high elevations, and this fresh olive leaf or branch was the indication to Noah that the water had receded from the earth.

Noah waited another seven days, and sent the dove out from the ark again. This time the dove did not return.

95

Expression: One day is as a thousand years

Location: 2 Peter 3:8

Verse: ... One day is with the Lord as a thousand years, and a
thousand years as one day.

In the writing of this scripture, Peter is not literally equating
one day and 1,000 years. This text is a figure of speech — a simile.

A similar text is from Psalm 90 which states: "For a thousand
years in thy sight are but as yesterday when it is past, and as a
watch in the night" (Psalm 90:4).

We are not to think that "yesterday" and "a thousand years" in
these instances are actually the same. This is simply a figure of
speech after studying it. This is not true of all scripture, of course,
where actual time is involved and is not being used figuratively.

In this verse from Second Peter, the main point is that time
means nothing to Eternal God. Our Eternal God is above and beyond the passage of time. Peter is explaining not the duration of a
day, but the timelessness of God.

96

Expression: One reaps what one sows

Location: Galatians 6:7

Verse: ... for whatsoever a man [person] soweth, that shall he [or she] also reap.

If a farmer plants cantaloupes, the farmer can expect to reap cantaloupes. Apricots will not come up. Likewise, if a person sows wrongful acts, that person can easily expect to reap problems, sorrow, and evil.

Even the apostle Paul learned this. Paul, before his conversion on the road to Damascus, was a leader in the stoning of Stephen. After Paul's conversion, when he was in the Galatian country, Paul too was stoned.

Every action has some kind of result.

97

Expression: Out of the mouth of babes

Location: Matthew 21:16

Verse: Out of the mouth of babes and sucklings [infants] thou hast
perfected praise.

Our dear little granddaughter had begun to say a few words.
She could say "ma ma," "da da," "baby," "car," "bus," and a few
other things which thrilled all of us. We would read books to her
and point out the picture of various animals. She could imitate the
sounds of many of them. She could go "moo," "bow-wow," buzz
like a bee, and chirp like a bird. Her best sound of an animal by far
was "baa" whenever she saw a little lamb.

One day as we were helping our daughter, son-in-law, and little
granddaughter move into their new home, the little one picked up
a part of a lamp and handed it to her grandmother. Grandmother
said, "That's part of a lamp."

Immediately, the little granddaughter gave out with a loud and
triumphant "baa!" She thought that she had heard the word "lamb."
Grandmother then said, "No, I said lamp. Light comes from the
lamp." Immediately, the little one said again with enthusiasm, "baa!"

The rest of us looked at each other and almost in unison said,
"Yes, the greatest light of all comes from a Lamb that sacrificed
his life on a cross for us."

Jesus told us, "I am the light of the world. Whoever follows me
will not walk in darkness, but will have the Light of life" (John
8:12, RSV).

98

Expression: The parting of the way

Location: Ezekiel 21:21

Verse: ... the king of Babylon stood at the parting of the way, at the head [fork] of the two ways [roads]....

This is a rather sad expression as we might use it today. When two business associates have a falling-out over a business deal, it is a shame that there comes the parting of the way.

A neighbor has to leave the community for good reasons, but there is a parting of the way, and all of the neighbors feel sadness.

The worst parting of all is when a husband and wife think they have to come to the parting of the way.

But in the scripture above, the expression is used with regard to which way to go.

There was one of two ways for Nebuchadnezzar, the king of Babylon, to follow. The king was uncertain whether to attack Jerusalem or Rabbah. He had come to the parting of the way.

99

Expression: **The patience of Job**

Location: James 5:11

Verse: Behold, we count them happy [blessed] which endure. Ye [you] have heard of the patience of Job....

Have you ever watched a teacher trained in special education at work? Have you seen the love and care that the teacher gives to a child whose body is twisted and pained? Have you observed the beautiful expression on the face of the child as well as the teacher?

This takes a special kind of person. One can easily say of these teachers, "They have the patience of Job."

Throughout this earthly life, all of us have often prayed for the patience of Job.

In the New Testament, the book of James cites Job from the Old Testament — Job who was especially persecuted, but also was enormously blessed.

Through Job's sorrow and afflictions, he stayed true to God; Job trusted the Lord. The rewards and blessings that eventually came to Job were enormous.

God's love and compassion endure.

100

Expression: A person after one's own heart

Location: Acts 13:22

Verse: And when he [God] had removed him [King Saul], he [God] raised up unto [for] them David to be their king; to whom also he gave testimony, and said, I have David the son of Jesse, a man after mine own heart, which shall fulfil all my will.

People like to be in the company of those with whom they can agree on certain ideas. If we hear a political speech from a person with whom we agree, it is very likely that we would say, "That is a person after my own heart."

If a judge announces a decision that people might agree with, they could easily say, "That judge is a person after my own heart."

The Bible also uses this expression. For instance, Paul and his companions on one of their preaching journeys went to Pisidian Antioch. On the sabbath day they entered the synagogue and sat down. During the worship they were invited to speak if they had a message of encouragement for the people.

Paul stood and began to relate the history of the Israelites. He told of their covenant with God, their bondage in Egypt, their plight of forty years in the desert, how God had given them judges to govern, then responded to the people's request for a king. God gave them their first king, Saul, son of Kish of the tribe of Benjamin, who ruled forty years. Then Paul related this scripture stated above concerning the next king, David.

101

Expression: Potter's field

Location: Matthew 27:7

Verse: And they took counsel, and bought with them [the money] the potter's field, to bury strangers in.

Wolfgang Amadeus Mozart has to be considered one of the most amazing child prodigies in history. By the age of six, he could play the harpsichord and violin. At age eight he wrote a symphony. When Mozart was only 35 years old, his health began to deteriorate. He was working on a requiem, a mass for the dead. Mozart rushed to finish it while on his own deathbed. He died shortly before his thirty-sixth birthday.

In view of his debts, Mozart received a pauper's funeral. His friends followed the hearse to his funeral, but when a violent storm came up on them, they turned back, leaving the hearse to proceed alone. With not a note of music, Mozart was placed in the common potter's field.

The expression "potter's field" has survived to this day to denote a burial place for strangers and the poor. The expression goes back some 2,000 years.

Judas Iscariot accepted thirty pieces of silver for turning over Jesus Christ to the chief priests of Jerusalem. After Judas realized the great sin that he had committed, he tried to give the money to the Temple. However, the chief priests and elders felt that the silver was unfit for Temple use. So with that money they bought a plot of land to be used as the "potter's field."

The term "potter's field" comes from the fact that clay was dug from the field and was used by artisans to mold their pottery.

102

Expression: **The powers that be**

Location: Romans 13:1

Verse: Let every soul [person] be subject unto the higher powers [governing authorities]. For there is no power but of God: the powers that be are ordained of God.

The frustrated employee spoke of many problems and conditions under which he had to work. His wife with loving concern made suggestions for possible improvement. The husband answered by saying, "But this is ordered by the powers that be."

Likewise, we often refer to the government as being "the powers that be" — the ones in control. The Bible speaks of this.

Many government authorities are evil and corrupt. However, believers have a responsibility to human government. God is still in control. History shows how a great government could flourish for a while and then be brought down in ruin.

People must be good citizens without compromising their beliefs in God.

103

Expression: A saint

Location: 2 Thessalonians 1:10

Verse: When he [Christ] shall come to be glorified in his saints, and to be admired in [among] all them that believe....

I always thought of my dear grandmother as a real saint. I believe that she had to be a notch above many others in the way she lived her life.

I shall never forget the terror that came over my young life when our family learned that Grandma had been struck by an automobile. We didn't know how badly she was hurt or any of the other details.

My mother, father, sister, and I quickly got ready and headed out for Grandma's house, where I so loved to play on the porch, pick up nuts off the ground, and stroll through the trees and listen to the birds. I sat in the car while we drove the ten miles to Grandma's house wondering, "How badly is she hurt?"

Thank God we soon arrived and learned that Grandma's leg had been hurt, but she really wasn't as bad off as we may have imagined during our drive to her home.

Grandma had been hit by a man in a pickup truck, and yes, the police had determined that the man had been drinking. The judge over the case ordered him to pay ten dollars per week to my grandma. Back in those days, ten dollars a week out of a man's pay was pretty rough.

Some members of the family were pleased that Grandma would be getting this help, and they definitely wanted her to take the money. My saintly grandmother didn't want to put a hardship on this man. Some of the family members told her she certainly should take the money at least until her medical bills were paid.

I shall never forget the pain on Grandma's face as she thought of taking money away from this man and his family. This grandmother saint of mine was filled with such love, compassion, and forgiveness that it broke her heart to think of taking this money. She did have to pay her medical bills though. Some of the family members insisted on that.

One day about five weeks later, we were at Grandma's house again when this man came to the door to pay her the weekly ten dollars. I looked on the face of this man who took his hat off and said, "How are you today, Mrs. Thompson?" I saw a man's face that revealed sincere politeness, humility, and great remorse. Over the weeks he had visited my grandmother, and probably for the first time in his life, he had met a person who was truly concerned about him. Later, I recall my grandmother told this gentleman that he didn't have to pay her ten dollars a week anymore.

I don't know what happened to this man, but I would like to believe that he became a child of God just from knowing my grandmother and seeing the Christian love that she had for him.

All of us have heard many times the word "saint" used in referring to someone who is enormously good in heart. All of my life I have been able to say about my grandma, "She was a saint."

My understanding of this expression was that the person referred to as a saint was much greater than normally "good." All of those years I understood the expression incorrectly. In going to the Bible — the Word of God — I read this scripture addressed to the Roman Christians by the apostle Paul: "To all that be in Rome, beloved of God, called to be saints [believers] ..." (Romans 1:7). Then after reading other passages, I looked up from my Bible and realized that the Bible refers to *all* Christian believers as "saints."

Yes, my grandma was a saint, and isn't it amazing what influence a saint can have over another person's life?

104

Expression: Salty talk

Location: Colossians 4:6

Verse: Let your speech be always with grace, seasoned with salt, that ye [you] may know how ye ought to answer every man [everyone].

Growing up I heard the expression "salty talk" many times, but to me it characterized some rather tough, even dirty, or maybe sarcastic language. It is not hard to find places where people are going to use a little bit of this salty talk. In fact, in some barbershops, if certain men are present, one's ears can tingle by their salty talk.

Once two good churchgoing friends played a trick on some men in a barbershop. One had gone there on a Monday to get a haircut. While he was in the barber's chair, this other good friend came in and sat down. They had a few kind words for each other, but mostly they were drowned out by several men who were armed for a full attack of "salt" on this day. They were using every vulgar word imaginable with every descriptive adjective in and out of the book.

The barber soon finished cutting the man's hair. As he got out of the chair, he looked at his friend and said, so that everyone could hear, "Pastor Jones, what did you preach on yesterday?" His friend quickly picked up on it and gave a good response.

That whole barbershop filled with men came to an instant, respectful, standstill silence. These two friends later had a big laugh about that incident.

But let's look at an expression about salty talk found in the Bible, which really takes on a different connotation. The passage is in the book of Colossians. The apostle Paul gave some very good advice to the church people in Colossae, which is stated above.

Does Paul imply here our definition of "salty talk"? No. In biblical times salt was considered a precious commodity. Salt is a preservative, and adds taste to food. Similarly, the Christian's conversation should be tasteful in making explanations about one's beliefs.

105

Expression: The scapegoat

Location: Leviticus 16:10

Verse: But the goat, on which the lot fell to be the scapegoat, shall be presented alive before the Lord, to make an atonement with [upon] him, and to let him go for [as] a scapegoat into the wilderness.

The headline on the morning newspaper read: "New Witness Made Scapegoat." It was interesting to see the newspaper was using a biblical term.

In a well-publicized court trial, the individual referred to in the headline was actually found to be not guilty, but he was being sacrificed as the scapegoat. Words were twisted so as to make this man appear guilty. He would take the blame for the real criminals in the case.

In the book of Leviticus, we read how the people of Israel began their annual ritual of the Day of Atonement known as Yom Kippur. On the tenth day of the seventh month, which was named Ethanim or Tishri on the Jewish calendar, and which approximates our present September/October, the high priest performed a ritual of atonement for his people. The high priest received two goats. The first goat was sacrificed as a sin offering, but on the head of the second goat, the high priest transferred all of the sins of the people by prayer. Afterward, this "scapegoat," bearing the people's sins, was released into the wilderness.

In the New Covenant, Jesus Christ is the scapegoat. The Lamb of God was sacrificed for the sins of the whole world. Christ who now lives is like the scapegoat which was sent away alive, removing the sins and the guilt of the people. This was not a ritual to be performed annually; rather it was a one-time sacrifice for the remission of sins for all the world for all eternity if we accept the gift and obey.

How do we define scapegoat today? The same. One who bears the blame for others.

106

Expression: See eye to eye

Location: Isaiah 52:8

Verse: Thy watchmen [sentinels] shall lift up the voice [their voices]; with the voice together shall they sing: for they shall see eye to eye, when the Lord shall bring again Zion.

When two people totally agree on a subject, we can say that they think alike, they are of one mind, or they see eye to eye.

Isaiah prophesied that God will someday restore Zion to its past glory. Isaiah refers to how beautiful upon the mountains it will be when the people on the watch will sing and shout for joy, as they will see right before their eyes God bringing his people home to Zion.

107

Expression: See how great a forest a little fire kindles

Location: James 3:5 (NKJV)

Verse: Even so the tongue is a little member [small part of the body], and boasts great things. See how great a forest a little fire kindles.

It was my first trip to the state of Oregon. I was delighted when some friends asked me to drive with them from Portland to the Pacific coast. I knew that I would see some beautiful country I had never seen before.

We drove through the land covered with tall, majestic trees reaching skyward almost like arms reaching toward heaven. I was assured of the vastness of this life in the forest.

All of a sudden, I was completely shocked when one of the men in the car rolled down his window and threw a lighted cigarette out. I couldn't help but be alarmed as I asked if he did not think that might catch the forest on fire.

Apparently I was the only one with this question on my mind as the others disregarded my statement, and the car sped on. I had my eye peeled for the next sight of a forest ranger.

We might think of the Oregon forest when we read this verse in the Bible. However, this scripture is comparing the fire to a person's uncontrolled, wicked, and vengeful words which can do just as much harm as a fire in a forest.

Many scholars place the teaching in the Epistle of James between A.D. 45 and 50; many believe it was written under the authority of the half-brother of Jesus.

In chapter three of this book of James, it speaks about the danger of the tongue, the uncontrolled language of the tongue. James states that we are capable of making a horse turn directions by a small bit in the horse's mouth. We are reminded that a tiny rudder on a ship can make the ship turn in whatever direction the pilot wants it to go.

The writer also states that a tongue is a small thing, but can do enormous damage if it is not controlled. In chapter three of James, we read the dramatic truism that a great forest with many trees can be set on fire by just a tiny spark. The tongue too can be a flame of wickedness.

When a tongue is under control, it can be a blessing. When a tongue is out of control, it is wicked, destructive, and even devastating to many.

108

Expression: **Separate the sheep from the goats**

Location: Matthew 25:32

Verse: And before him [the Lord] shall be gathered all nations: and he shall separate them [people] one from another, as a shepherd divideth his sheep from the goats.

It was the end of the spring practice, and each member of the football team nervously stood and listened as the coach was ready to read the cut. Today the coach was going to separate the sheep from the goats. Some players would qualify, and some would not.

The Bible speaks of this also. When it is time to judge the nations of the world, the Lord will separate the righteous from the unrighteous. Sheep are the righteous, and goats are the unrighteous. As my pastor says, "Sheep can be led, but goats have to be driven." Sheep and goats often grazed together out in the field, but they were separated when it came time to shear the sheep.

109

Expression: Shout for joy

Location: Psalm 5:11

Verse: But let all those that put their trust in thee rejoice: let them ever shout for joy....

A young lady rushed into the church choir room. She had a broad smile on her face, and her friends heard her say, "I could shout for joy!"

The whole room of people became a more cheerful place with the entrance of this happy person. The words "I could shout for joy" made everyone exuberant for the moment.

It would have been wonderful if her expression had been caused by something she had just heard or studied in her church school class. But her friends had to be content that she was referring to a very big football game played the night before. Of course, everyone still celebrated her joy that her team had won.

We have heard many say that they "shouted for joy" when something good came into their lives. This expression is found in the Bible many times, too.

The Bible tells us that the greatest joy in one's life is following the laws of God and having God direct our lives. The beautiful songs found in the book of Psalms utilize this joy often. Another short excerpt is: "Let them shout for joy, and be glad, that favor my righteous cause ... (Psalm 35:27).

110

Expression: **Signs of the times**

Location: Matthew 16:3

Verse: ... O ye hypocrites, ye can discern [interpret] the face [appearance] of the sky; but can ye not discern the signs of the times?

We have heard business people say when profits are up or profits are down, "Oh, it's just the signs of the times."

While sitting in an office waiting to see one of his church members, the pastor began to thumb through a magazine which he found on the table. This good friend was in the sign-making business. In a moment the pastor realized that the magazine he had picked up was called *Signs of the Times*. (This is a very attractive magazine for the sign industry published by ST Publications, Inc., in Cincinnati, Ohio.)

The gentleman with whom the pastor had this appointment was a Christian, so it was not at all unusual that a Bible was on the table there with the magazines. While the pastor waited, he picked up the Bible and opened it to the book of Matthew. To his surprise, he opened it to a page on which was the expression, "signs of the times." He began to reflect on this as he read.

What is meant by this expression? One day Jesus was approached by the Pharisees and the Sadducees. These were Jewish politico-religious leaders of two different parties. These men tried to test Jesus' claim of being the Messiah by asking him to show them some great sign from heaven. They wanted to trap Jesus.

The Lord had provided these men with many signs, but they would not accept them. They were eyewitnesses to the fulfillment of literally hundreds of Old Testament prophecies concerning the first coming of the Messiah, but they could not interpret the "signs of the times." The Pharisees and Sadducees considered Jesus an imposter and did not believe he was the Messiah. The multitudes thought that Jesus was John the Baptist, Elijah, Jeremiah, or some other prophet. However, Jesus' disciples believed that he was the Messiah, the Christ, the Son of the Living God.

Jesus was aware of the motives of these leaders who had approached him. So Jesus first responded to them by telling them that they were good at reading the signs of the weather. When they saw a red sky at night, they believed it would mean fair weather the next day. When they saw a red sky in the morning, they predicted foul weather all day. But Jesus told them that they couldn't read the obvious signs of the times. They were not able to see the truth surrounding the Lord Jesus who had come to save the world.

111

Expression: **Smoother than butter**

Location: Psalm 55:21

Verse: The words of his mouth were smoother than butter, but war was in his heart....

Our present day doesn't have sole possession of the con artist ("con" standing for "confidence"). The con artist has been around for a long time.

What other names can we give to a con? How about deceiver, swindler, sharpie, shark, phony, and charlatan? How about hypocrite? And let's hazard that all of them speak a line smoother than butter.

In Psalm 55, David is finding that the tongue is as deadly as a drawn sword in battle.

112

Expression: Some to honor and some to dishonor

Location: 2 Timothy 2:20

Verse: But in a great house there are not only vessels of gold and of silver, but also of wood and of earth [clay]; and some to honor [for noble use], and some to dishonor [hold cheap].

Dr. Madison Sarratt, who taught mathematics at Vanderbilt University for many years, would admonish his class before a test: "Today I'm giving two exams — one in trigonometry and the other in honesty. I hope you pass both of them. If you must fail one, fail trigonometry. There are many good people in the world who can't pass trig, but none who can't pass the test of honesty." The Bible says this also.

The scripture above is from a letter that the apostle Paul wrote to the young preacher, Timothy. This was probably written around A.D. 67 while Paul was in prison. Paul was writing Timothy encouraging him to continue his training in serving his congregation. Paul at this time was about sixty years old, and he was sharing his insights and wisdom from over thirty years in the ministry.

In this particular verse, the message is given with the analogy of a household's utensils. Some of the utensils in the household are valuable and are used with great honor. Others are cheap, and are used in less than noble ways — maybe used to collect the garbage.

Paul is saying that we here on earth are to be servants or vessels also. We can be used by God if we will separate ourselves from the dishonorable and evil around us. We can become a vessel or utensil for honor —   prepared to do any good work.

113

Expression: **Sour grapes**

Location: Ezekiel 18:2

Verse: What mean ye, that ye use this proverb concerning the land of Israel, saying, The fathers [parents] have eaten sour grapes [sinned], and the children's teeth are set on edge?

A student enrolling in Psychology 101 will probably have a big discussion on rationalization in class. A person can rationalize by justifying or setting up a defense mechanism. If a person finds disparagement of something that has proven unattainable, the person will probably say, "Oh, I didn't want it anyway." That is sour grapes.

In the scripture above, "sour grapes" means sin. The people of Judah believed that they were being punished for the sins of their ancestors. The prophet Ezekiel helped to set them straight on this matter.

God judges each person individually. We often suffer from the effects of sins committed by those who came before us. But each person will receive personal judgment for each person's personal conduct.

114

Expression: Spare the rod and spoil the child

Location: Proverbs 13:24 (NRSV)

Verse: Those who spare the rod hate their children, but those who
love them are diligent to discipline them.

How many parents over the years have used this expression as
they discipline their children, "knowing" that they are right? Most
know that this comes from the Bible. This is the reason they feel
that they have the permission to "wail the daylights" out of their
kids. Yes, it is in the Bible, but it may not mean exactly what a lot
of people think.

This expression is in the book of Proverbs, but this attitude of
discipline is not only in the Old Testament. For instance, in the
New Testament book of Hebrews, chapter 12, we read that God is
our Father, and God corrects us and teaches us as a loving father.

Again in the New Testament we read: "And, ye fathers, provoke not your children to wrath [making them resentful]: but bring
them up in the nurture [training] and admonition [instruction] of
the Lord [with suggestions and godly advice]" (Ephesians 6:4).

Aristotle wrote: "It is more a human characteristic to be able to
defend oneself with speech and reason than by means of physical
force."

Albert Einstein stated: "Violence may have cleared away obstructions quickly, but it never has proved itself creative."

It seems reasonable to believe that physically hitting a child is
not the most effective way to maintain discipline. We should consider nonviolent behavior management techniques. We should realize that hitting a child is a very effective way to teach that child
to be violent. The child can lose self-respect and lose heart.

Teachers can testify that good classroom discipline is neces-
sary for students' learning. Good discipline is maintained through

a climate of order and respect. Learning takes place in an unthreatened environment.

In the Bible scripture from Proverbs, let us consider the word "rod" as a figure of speech signifying discipline of any type. So instead of saying, "Spare the rod and spoil the child," let us substitute for the word "rod" such phrases as: training, guidance, advice, teaching, wisdom, correction, love, understanding, and being a good example.

115

Expression: The spirit is willing, but the flesh is weak

Location: Matthew 26:41

Verse: ... the spirit indeed is willing, but the flesh is weak.

It was a holiday. The company employees had just finished a delicious dinner in the home of their boss. Following dinner the host brought out four different kinds of candy to serve everyone. Many declined the offer as they said that they had been trying to hold to more nutritious meals. The host was quite obese and in no way needed to continue eating, especially candy. As the boss took for himself two handfuls of the assorted confections, he said with a laugh, "I shouldn't do this. The spirit is willing, but the flesh is weak."

How many times have we heard this expression? Jesus was aware of our weaknesses, too. In the book of Matthew, we are reminded of the sorrowful time when our Lord used this expression. It was after Jesus and his disciples had eaten the Last Supper in the Upper Room that Jesus took several disciples to the Garden of Gethsemane. Jesus took Peter, James, and John and asked them to be with him, and to stay awake while he prayed. But after Jesus finished praying, he found the disciples asleep. He asked Peter why he couldn't stay awake with him just an hour and pray. He reminded Peter that without prayer, temptation would overcome him. Jesus reminded Peter that the spirit is willing, but the flesh is weak.

On many occasions we want to do the right thing, but our human nature tempts us, and we give in.

116

Expression: **Stick out your tongue**

Location: Isaiah 57:4 (NRSV)

Verse: Whom are you mocking? Against whom do you open your mouth wide and stick out your tongue? Are you not children of transgression, the offspring of deceit [liars]?

As children, where did we learn to stick out our tongues at others we didn't like? How did we learn to stick out our tongues at someone who had done something to us of which we did not approve? Where did we develop the idea that sticking out our tongues was a form of protest? Why did we always associate sticking out our tongues at someone as being disapproving?

I am not about to suggest that this got its start from reading the Bible. I'm not suggesting that it didn't either. I just don't know.

From chapter 57 of the book of Isaiah, the writer is speaking to the offspring of adulterers and harlots involved in spiritual adultery and idolatry.

117

Expression: Stiffnecked

Location: Acts 7:51

Verse: Ye stiffnecked [people] and uncircumcised in heart and ears, ye do always resist [oppose] the Holy Ghost [Spirit]: as your fathers [ancestors] did, so do ye.

In biblical times, the ox was used to plow fields and pull carts. Oxen were stubborn and hard to manage. When an ox would stiffen the muscles in its neck, it was very difficult to guide.

Stiffnecked is an expression to identify people who are defiant, stubborn, and willful as oxen.

Circumcision in the Old Testament can literally mean the physical operation. Circumcision in the New Testament often refers to the change in a person's heart — the change for purity and faith as believers in the Lord.

This Bible statement was made by Stephen in his address before the council prior to being stoned to death. Stephen told the council that they did not obey God any more than their ancestors had down through the years.

118

Expression: A still small voice

Location: 1 Kings 19:11-12

Verse: ... Go forth, and stand upon the mount before [in the presence of] the Lord. And, behold, the Lord passed by, and a great and strong wind rent [split] the mountains, and brake in pieces the rocks before the Lord; but the Lord was not in the wind: and after the wind an earthquake; but the Lord was not in the earthquake: And after the earthquake a fire; but the Lord was not in the fire: and after the fire a still small voice.

I remember most of my teachers I had in school. As a small child one can adore one's teachers or have fear of them.

I can recall two of my teachers in particular. They were extreme opposites. One lady had a loud and rough voice. She was large in size and fairly tall. She had a very dominating manner. All of her students were afraid of her. When our class made some noise, the teacher's voice would crescendo to a greater volume and would rise to a higher pitch. This action didn't help the class to become quiet; it made the general sound of the class get louder.

Then there was Miss Ethel. She was small in stature, very refined, and her facial expressions seemed always to be loving. I liked Miss Ethel. The main things I remember about her were her smile and her still small voice.

I have heard many people in conversation make a reference to "a still small voice." Many probably are not aware of the fact that the expression comes from the Bible.

In First Kings we read of the magnificent ministry and exciting escapades of Elijah. In chapter 19 the Lord makes himself known to Elijah. The great prophet Elijah had been very zealous for the Lord God Almighty. The Israelites had rejected the covenant of God, destroyed the altars of the Lord, and put some of God's prophets to death. Elijah was one left to stand up boldly against the prophets of Baal. Elijah too feared for his life. Then the word of the Lord came to Elijah.

At one point the scripture states that sometimes the word of God comes by spectacular demonstrations of power, wind, earthquake, or fire. But the word of God can come also through a still small voice.

Many centuries later this was to be found in a perfect example of the still small voice of Christ in the hearts of humankind.

119

Expression: The straight and narrow

Location: Matthew 7:13-14

Verse: For wide is the gate, and broad [easy] is the way, that leadeth to destruction, and many there be which go in thereat: Because strait [hard] is the gate, and narrow is the way, which leadeth unto life, and few there be that find it.

"The straight and narrow" has become in present-day language an expression describing the road of righteousness for the life of a person.

I have fond memories of my years of being active in the Boy Scouts. We experienced some exciting moments when we would launch our canoes out onto the scenic Harpeth River on the outskirts of Nashville.

The river varied in its width as we traveled downstream. As the river curved and snaked its way below the overhanging magnolia trees, we would often find ourselves paddling our canoes through some very narrow sections of the river while dodging the rocks. In fact, there is one place on the river which is known as "The Narrows" at the old Montgomery Bell property.

It was easy to move our canoes through the water at the broad parts of the river. Some of us would get a little lax in observing how we operated our canoes. But, when we got to the narrow sections of the river, we worked hard to maneuver our canoes properly. At that time, we became more serious, dedicated, unselfish, devoted, and committed. And, we found success.

In these verses from Matthew, Jesus tells us that the gateway to eternal life is very narrow. Jesus also tells us that he is the gate (John 10:7).

120

Expression: **Strain at a gnat and swallow a camel**

Location: Matthew 23:24

Verse: Ye blind guides, which strain at [out] a gnat, and swallow a camel.

There was a time when Jesus had to scold the religious leaders of his day. Some of them were tremendously concerned about making a federal case of many trifles, yet accepting some major defects without complaining. So Jesus spoke these words.

Some scribes and Pharisees would carefully strain their drinking water through a cloth so as not to swallow an unclean gnat. But they would swallow something huge like a camel, meaning figuratively that they would overlook large and important matters such as justice, mercy, and faith.

121

Expression: **A stumbling block**

Location: Ezekiel 3:20

Verse: ... When a righteous man [person] doth turn from his [or her] righteousness, and commit iniquity [does evil], and I lay a stumblingblock before him [that person], he [or she] shall die....

One was heard saying, "Don't do that! You could be a stumbling block to that person." That could also be said about certain movies and television shows.

What a person says and does may affect the life of someone else. A role model should feel a responsibility for someone weaker who may fall away from goodness. Love for the weaker person should prevent us from doing something that could lead that person into doing evil.

The apostle Paul warns us of the influence by example upon another person. We need to be responsible. To cause another person to sin is quite serious. One should not be an obstacle or stumbling block.

Paul stressed that it is the love for others that helps the buildup of the community.

122

Expression: Sweeter than honey

Location: Psalm 19:10

Verse: More to be desired are they than gold, yea, than much fine
gold: sweeter also than honey and the honeycomb.

"They" in the verse, which the psalmist is saying are so desired,
are such things as the law of the Lord, the decrees of the Lord, the
precepts and commandments of the Lord, and God's righteousness.

The psalmist is saying that the observance of God's laws is a
joy, not a burden. God's laws are pure, eternal, and just. They de-
liver us from harm, and they point at success and guide us. They
are sweeter than honey.

123

Expression: **Take it to heart**

Location: Isaiah 57:1 (NRSV)

Verse: The righteous perish, and no one takes it to heart.

I began teaching school when I was a young man in my twenties. I was lucky to have the opportunity to teach in a school under a very strong principal and with a very good faculty. Back in those days, the schools were smaller, and there was a very good rapport between the students and faculty. Teachers didn't work at that profession for great financial gain. If that had been our objective, we would have been grossly disappointed. The motivation was a sincere desire to teach, to help others develop, to be a good witness and role model for the youth, and to counsel those who needed help whether it be physical, mental, or moral in nature.

The principal of our school was loved by everyone. He was a fine disciplinarian, respected by students as well as faculty. In my first year of teaching when I was having a discipline problem, the principal was capable of offering me excellent advice.

Our principal had an expression he used often. When he explained something, he would conclude by saying, "Take it to heart." When he disciplined a student, he would conclude with the expression, "Take it to heart."

This is good advice. When people say this, they are really saying: "Listen to what I say. Believe what I say. Hold this message close to your heart, which is the most delicate, sensitive, and spiritual part of one's body."

We find this expression in the book of Isaiah.

124

Expression: Take under one's wing

Location: Luke 13:34

Verse: ... how often would I have gathered thy children together, as a hen doth gather her brood under her wings....

There was an endearing schoolteacher in the one-room school out in the country. On a cold, wintry day, this teacher could be seen with her children out on the playground. She would take her great shawl and spread it out over several small children to protect them from the cold.

A newspaper reporter writing a story about this wonderful teacher made the statement, "She appeared as a loving mother hen protecting the children under her wing."

The Bible gives this same description about the Lord. This is one of the times that the Lord is referred to as a mother figure. The Lord is compared to a hen gathering her young safely under her wing.

125

Expression: **Teeth set on edge**

Location: Jeremiah 31:29-30

Verse: In those days they shall say no more, The fathers [ances-
tors] have eaten a sour grape, and the children's teeth are
set on edge. But every one shall die for his [her] own iniquity [sin]: every man [whoever] that eateth the sour grape,
his [her] teeth shall be set on edge.

I presume it is a physical impossibility to have your teeth set on
edge. But this expression has been used by many for years. When
the teacher accidentally scraped her fingernails across the chalkboard, the student cringed and said, "That sets my teeth on edge."

It doesn't have to take a noise to bring on this expression, either. One person was telling about a serious auto wreck. The details of the tragedy were so vivid that the listener said, "That sets
my teeth on edge."

This expression is found in the Bible. These two verses from
the prophet Jeremiah are saying that the people will no longer quote
the old saying about children paying for their parents' sins, but that
people will die for their own sins. The person eating the sour grapes
[the one who sins] will be the one whose teeth are set on edge.

126

Expression: There is no God

Location: Psalm 14:1

Verse: The fool hath said in his [her] heart, There is no God. They are corrupt, they have done abominable works, there is none that doeth good.

Many of us remember the so-called theologian a good many years back who espoused the "God-is-dead" movement. All of us have heard an atheist on a radio or television talk show who was so positive of being right that he or she emphatically said, "There is no God."

Many years ago we heard the report of the Russian astronauts who returned from space, and with a smile expressed words to the effect that they had been up in the heavens and they didn't see any God up there. All of us have heard at some time or other the words, "There is no God."

It actually hurts me, and even sets my teeth on edge, to put these blasphemous words in print. However, we find this expression in the Bible.

The Bible tells us that wickedness of people's pride prevents them from seeking God. They have no room for God in their thoughts.

Believers in God know that there will come a day of judgment for the wicked and the people who do not believe in God. But believers can look forward to the day of judgment as a day of joy for their own lives.

127

Expression: There is no peace for the wicked

Location: Isaiah 48:22

Verse: There is no peace, saith the Lord, unto [for] the wicked.

My wife and I helped our daughter and son-in-law move into a new house. We have had experience, for in our younger days we did our share of moving.

During the moves we were able to clear out things that we no longer needed. We always organized our material wealth in three categories. There were things we would throw away, there were things we would give away, and there were things we would sell. It was always fun to load up the items to give away, which would benefit the church, Salvation Army, Goodwill Industries, or some other worthy organization.

I can still remember the hard work involved. I would always appreciate the night when I could lie down and rest. More than once I can recall my wife, in the midst of our hard work, declaring that old expression: "There is no peace for the wicked."

We got another good taste of that hard work when we helped our daughter and son-in-law move. Would you believe, as the day wore on, my daughter, who looks and sounds like my wife, was heard from the kitchen exclaiming with a sound of desperate pain and frustration, "There is no peace for the wicked!"

As we continue to read in the book of Isaiah, we find that the nation Israel in its time of sin and disobedience is being reminded of God's promises. Israel was disobedient. The people worshiped idols. They were sinful, greedy, doing everything their evil hearts desired. God through his prophets constantly was trying to bring his people back to truth and salvation. But, the scripture says, "... the wicked are like the troubled sea, when it cannot rest, whose waters cast up mire and dirt. There is no peace, saith my God, to [for] the wicked" (Isaiah 57:20-21).

Throughout all the prophecies of warning and preparing the people of Israel, God interweaves the thread of hope — the coming of the Messiah. Isaiah promises the people that the coming Messiah will bring them into a loving relationship with God eventually.

128

Expression: **There is none righteous, no, not one**

Location: Romans 3:9-10

Verse: ... we have before proved [made the charge] both Jews and Gentiles, that they are all under sin [under sin's power and condemnation], as it is written, There is none righteous, no, not one.

Possibly you have heard your grandparents use this expression. It is in the Bible. What does it say to us?

Rome in the year A.D. 56 was the center of one of the greatest empires this world has ever known. The Emperor ruled over the Roman Empire of approximately a million people. A tiny portion of this population was called Christians. The apostle Paul wrote many letters to the brothers and sisters in Christianity, and one was to the Christian community in Rome.

In chapter 3 of this epistle, Paul explains that all are guilty — Jews and Gentiles alike. However, Paul explains that God's new plan by way of Jesus Christ, the New Covenant, will bring us the righteousness we need — righteousness through faith by which we can be saved.

Not being righteous means not being right or good. It means no one is innocent. We have to be right according to God's laws. We need to play by God's rules. We have the free choice of asking for salvation and living the joy of eternity with our Lord, or not being saved.

God is telling us that this is his universe. We are living in his world. We use God's sunshine, water, and air. And God tells us through his Holy Word, the Bible, that he has worked out a plan for us wicked to be saved. We are sinners, but God wants to save us and make us happy, because he created us and he loves us.

Now we know God's plan. We can take it or leave it.

129

Expression: There is nothing new under the sun

Location: Ecclesiastes 1:9 (NRSV)

Verse: What has been is what will be, and what has been done is what will be done; there is nothing new under the sun.

A man and wife from the Midwest had the opportunity to visit some dear friends in a distant southern state. They had not seen this couple for many years. Their visit allowed them to have wonderful talks about the good old days. They enjoyed reliving many happy experiences through their memories.

The couple being visited were very interested in a new manufacturing company that had been established in their town. The man had been appointed the director of personnel over this whole company, and his wife was a very wonderful help to him as they had to organize, hire, and set up the whole organization and administration of this new establishment.

This hard-working couple wouldn't let their friends leave after a few days' visit. They insisted that they stay a full week. Being the director of personnel of this large company, the man got clearance for their friends to have a guided tour of this plant.

The tour took almost a full day. The thing that kept being impressed on them as they were shown all of the manufacturing processes was that the modern technology was based on old processes. The host was an excellent teacher. He would show them a very high-tech process and then back it up with some knowledge of how it "used to be done." Actually, the old, time-tested procedures were still in use, but slightly modified or altered to incorporate an electrical, mechanical, or high-tech process offering more efficiency.

After a delightful day of touring and learning, it could be estimated that at least ten times during the day the host expressed, "So you see, there is nothing new under the sun."

The wisdom of Solomon allowed him to write this very expression. In the book of Ecclesiastes, Solomon wrote that generations pass on, nature continues in the same way, but nothing new results.

130

Expression: They who follow vain persons will have poverty enough

Location: Proverbs 28:19

Verse: He [one] that tilleth [plows] his [one's] land shall have plenty of bread: but he [one] that followeth after vain persons [worthless pursuits or frivolity] shall have poverty enough.

It is displeasing to hear people speak in an uncomplimentary tone about their in-laws. There was a woman who would get to the subject of her in-laws no matter what the conversation.

Her church pastor saw this bitter, caustic, unhappy woman on the street one day. They began to talk about an upcoming program at the local high school. Soon the woman remarked: "If that no count son-in-law of mine had spent more time studying in high school rather than running around so much, he could be making a lot better living for his wife and family right now."

She concluded by saying, "But, as the Proverb says, 'He who follows vain persons shall have poverty enough.' "

The pastor walked away from this encounter thinking, "I wish that lady knew as much about other Bible scripture as she seems to know what Proverbs has to say about her son-in-law."

This scripture from Proverbs says that the one who works will have abundant food, but the one who chases fantasies or schemes for making easy money will have plenty of poverty.

God is telling us to stay on the job, keep busy, and don't get sidetracked with the wrong people and the wrong objectives. We need to keep our minds trained on what the Lord's will is for our lives.

131

Expression: A thorn in the flesh

Location: 2 Corinthians 12:7

Verse: ... there was given to me a thorn in the flesh, the [a] messenger of Satan to buffet [torment] me, lest I should be exalted above measure.

Three college students set out to do some home improvement work during one summer to make money for their college tuition. They were hired to do some work at the home of a woman who wanted the students to put a brick trim down both sides of her driveway.

One student would shovel out the dirt, mix the mortar, haul the brick, and put a level on the brick as they worked. The other two guys did the creative job of building the perfect and attractive line of bricks. At least, it was supposed to be perfect and attractive.

It was often hard for the students to work because the owner would stand by and constantly tell them that a brick was not even, or it was not straight, or one brick didn't match the next.

The students tried to be courteous, polite, and helpful. They tried desperately to please her, but they were not too sure of how well they accomplished any of that. One morning when they came to work, one said, "That lady is a thorn in my flesh." This expression has been said over the years when a person gains a burden or problem.

The apostle Paul talked about his "thorn" in Second Corinthians. God blessed Paul in so many ways. Paul was even given a vision of Paradise. But Paul states that God's will was to keep him humble. Paul knew that God's grace was sufficient for his burden. Paul stated that when he was weak, God's glory and power were strong.

We do not know for certain what Paul's "thorn" was. It is believed by many to be chronic ophthalmia, which is a disease of the eyes, and which made Paul offensive in appearance. For instance,

Paul wrote that even though his affliction probably was revolting to people, they didn't reject him and turn him away (Galatians 4:14). Paul continues that he knew that they would gladly have taken out their own eyes and given them to replace his if that would have helped him (Galatians 4:15).

The book of Galatians speaks of Paul's large handwriting, which may have been due to poor eyesight. Paul states that he would write the closing words in his own handwriting and speaks of how large he has to make the letters (Galatians 6:11).

It is suggested by some that the Holy Spirit suppressed the exact information in the Bible regarding Paul's infirmities in order that sufferers of a wide variety of "thorns" might find in Paul's experience the comfort and grace they need. Paul's teaching should help all to live and flourish with their "thorns."

Paul prayed for his "thorn" to be removed. God'answer to Paul's prayer was "No!" It kept Paul humble, and it reminded him that he needed to keep in close touch with God. Paul's "thorn" benefited people around him as they saw God at work in his life.

Paul had the correct response with regard to his infirmities. It is the response each of us should have when we are asked to live with our infirmities. Paul said: "... Most gladly therefore will I rather glory in my infirmities [weakness], that the power of Christ may rest upon me" (2 Corinthians 12:9).

We will settle for the power of Christ, won't we?

132

Expression: **Till death do us part**

Location: Ruth 1:16-17

Verse: And Ruth said, Entreat me not to leave thee, or to return [turn away] from following after thee: for whither thou goest, I will go; and where thou lodgest [live], I will lodge: thy people shall be my people, and thy God my God. Where thou diest, will I die, and there will I be buried: the Lord do so to me, and more also, if aught but death part thee and me.

Naomi was an Israelite woman who had seen her husband and two sons die while in Moab during the famine. Ruth, a Gentile, was Naomi's daughter-in-law who chose to stay with Naomi on her return to Judah. This was the ultimate expression of great love, devotion, and faithfulness to another human being.

The marriage vow from *The Book of Common Prayer* states: "To have and to hold from this day forward, for better for worse, for richer for poorer, in sickness and in health, to love and to cherish, till death do us part."

133

Expression: **To be all things to all people**

Location: 1 Corinthians 9:22

Verse: ... I [Paul] am made all things to all men [people], that I might by all means save some.

Many people of this world attempt to be all things to all people. Unfortunately, often their aims and goals are not led by righteousness.

The politician was willing to lie, cheat, and become corrupt to achieve certain end goals. The high school student seemed to change his personality completely as he mixed first with one group of his peers, and later with another. The lawyer was willing to misrepresent and mislead in order to win the court case by being all things to all people.

In chapter 9 of First Corinthians, the apostle Paul says that he dealt with different people in different ways in order to win their souls to God. When Paul was among Jews, he became like one under the law of Moses. Of course, Paul never committed a sin when mixing with others and trying to fit in. When with Gentiles who had not been reared under the Old Testament law, Paul accommodated himself to Gentile culture — of course, only when it did not violate his allegiance to God.

When Paul was with heathen, he didn't argue with them. Instead, he hoped to win their confidence and thereby help them to learn about God.

When Paul was with those who were weak, he didn't act as though he knew it all, and he didn't call them names. It is hoped that the result was that the people were willing to have Paul help them.

This is how Paul tried to be all things to all people.

134

Expression: **To every thing there is a season**

Location: Ecclesiastes 3:1

Verse: To every thing there is a season, and a time to every purpose under the heaven.

A grandfather was strolling with his granddaughter in the park. They were talking as they leisurely walked. The beautiful autumn colors had begun to blanket the leaves of the trees with their bright oranges, brilliant reds, and gorgeous yellows.

The grandfather began to talk about the changing seasons. Then there came an exchange of short questions and answers.

Grandfather said, "What happens in the fall?"

Granddaughter quickly said, "We start back to school."

Grandfather: "What happens in the winter?"

Granddaughter used a quick and short answer, "Snow."

Grandfather: "What happens in the spring?"

After a moment the granddaughter responded with, "April showers bring May flowers."

Following a slight chuckle, Grandfather asked, "And, what happens in the summer?"

With bright eyes, the granddaughter raised her voice slightly and said, "We go swimming, have picnics, and play ball."

There is a time, a divinely appointed time, for everything, and a season for every activity under the heaven. Our lives are governed by God's perfect and faithful timing.

135

Expression: **Turn the other cheek**

Location: Matthew 5:39

Verse: But I say unto you that ye resist not evil [an evil person]: but whosoever shall smite thee on thy right cheek, turn to him [that evildoer] the other also.

The expression "turn the other cheek" is used by Jesus in his Sermon on the Mount where he states the principles that characterize the Kingdom of Heaven.

What does this mean?

The emphasis is on maintaining an attitude of perfect love toward one's enemies as well as one's friends. Even if acts of violence are committed, no revenge should be taken. Enmity on the part of others should always stimulate a believer in God to greater manifestations of love. Naturally, our Lord does not advocate a weak and sentimental attitude toward evildoers. Jesus teaches that hatred should never be repaid with hatred but with true, unselfish love. Genuine love under the guidance of the Holy Spirit will always do what is best for the enemy.

While on a preaching trip across Poland, a pastor met some other pastors there who had gone through terrible abuse and persecution during a prior Communist administration. He reported that these Christians never reviled their enemies. Some of the men had scar tissue on their backs that was horrible to see.

This visiting pastor joyfully reported that a former Communist party chief in Poland who severely oppressed the Christians is now on the staff in one of the churches. Because of the love and concern of those Christian pastors, that man is now a born-again, Spirit-filled minister of the gospel.

Believers are a part of the Kingdom of God. Jesus expects them to turn the other cheek. This is unnatural. Only God can give one the strength to do this. Christian conduct should never betray the high moral standards of the gospel, or it very well will provoke the disdain of unbelievers and bring the gospel into disrepute.

136

Expression: Two are better than one

Location: Ecclesiastes 4:9

Verse: Two are better than one; because they have a good reward [return] for their labor [work].

Did you know that there are some oil wells in southern Indiana and southern Illinois? When we lived in Indiana, a good friend of mine who was a geologist drilled an oil well. He began to make money from it right away. He told me how many barrels of oil it was pumping, and then said, "If I had good sense, I would drill a second oil well and make twice the amount of money."

I recall another friend in that same town who was a very successful insurance agent. He told me that he was working himself to death, but if he put a second person on the other side of town, then they could cover twice the amount of territory.

In a recent meeting at a church, the devotional by a member was referring to Jesus sending his disciples out in "twos" to serve and minister. Jesus knew that they would be more successful that way. In this man's devotional, he quoted the scripture in the Gospel according to Mark that states that Jesus called unto him the twelve disciples and began to send them forth two by two (Mark 6:7).

Following this devotional, the members at the meeting decided to send their people out in twos to the homes in the community to encourage some of their friends who were not attending church to come and worship.

We also find this expression under consideration in the book of Ecclesiastes where Solomon states that two can support each other and lend help in time of trouble.

137

Expression: A two-edged sword

Location: Revelation 1:16

Verse: And he had in his right hand seven stars: and out of his mouth went a sharp two-edged sword....

"This is a two-edged sword," expressed the new pastor who had just taken over a small church in the community.

The meeting of a church committee was expressing the need for more members. The pastor stated that the present problem was that it would be difficult to enroll new members until there was an exciting program to present to the people. And it would be difficult to develop a strong program until there were more people involved to participate. Thus the basis of the pastor's statement, "This is a two-edged sword."

The book of Revelation was written after 90 A.D. by John, who at this time had been exiled to the island of Patmos. Patmos is an island in the Aegean Sea, about sixty miles southwest of Ephesus, and about 150 miles east of Athens, Greece. The island is ten miles long, six miles wide, treeless and rocky.

While there, John saw Jesus in many visions and was told by Jesus to write things down which would become part of the Bible. During the visions, John saw Jesus with a two-edged sword.

In Revelation 1:16, the seven stars represent the seven churches to which John was to write letters through the dictation of Jesus. The sword symbolizes the Word of God in divine judgment. (See Isaiah 49:2.)

138

Expression: Vanity, all is vanity

Location: Ecclesiastes 1:2

Verse: Vanity of vanities, saith the Preacher, vanity of vanities; all is vanity.

Have you ever been bored beyond words when you have had to sit in a doctor's office to wait your turn?

The last time I was in a doctor's office, I tried to relieve my boredom by reading the newspaper, then reading a magazine. I strolled down the hall to get a drink of water. Still my name was not called. Finally, I decided to relax and just watch the other people around me. Up to this time, I had not even been aware of another person speaking.

One lady was noticeable in that she was fidgety. She went into her purse many times, and on each occasion she would bring out her mirror and look at herself, fix her hair, primp, put the mirror away, get it back out, on and on. Of course, she had every right in the world to do that. However, one woman much older in years couldn't take it much longer. She began to mumble under her breath. Finally, I heard her say, "Vanity, all is vanity!"

A class of high school sophomores was involved in vocabulary and the true meanings of words. The word "vanity" came up. Before you read on, what word or phrase would you use to define "vanity"?

On this particular occasion with this class of sophomores, the teacher went to the chalkboard and said, "Give me words or phrases to define 'vanity' until we have arrived at a list of nine."

You may be interested in seeing the nine that these young people came up with: vain, futile, idle, empty, meaningless, worthless, excessively proud, self-conceited, and fruitless.

After the list was made, one student asked the teacher what word or phrase he would use. That was only fair. The teacher

173

answered his request by saying that the word "vanity" reminded him of "Vanity Fair" in Bunyan *Pilgrim's Progress.* A fair always going on in the town of Vanity was symbolic of worldly folly, frivolity, and show.

Vanity [meaninglessness] is the theme of the book of Ecclesiastes. The word "vanity" occurs over thirty times.

Thought to be written by King Solomon about 940 B.C., Ecclesiastes reveals that only a life lived in relationship with God's great wisdom is a life that is fulfilled.

139

Expression: **Vengeance is the Lord's**

Location: Romans 12:19

Verse: Dearly beloved, avenge not yourselves, but rather give place unto wrath [so far as anger goes]: for it is written, Vengeance is mine; I will repay, saith the Lord.

A man was being interviewed on a talk show in a television studio. The host of the show first had the man tell his story to the audience. This fellow reported that his home had been broken into when he was not at home. His wife and five-year-old daughter were in the home at the time. The intruder tied the man's wife to a chair and made her watch while he raped her sweet, little five-year-old child.

As this man's story progressed, the audience at the television taping almost became unruly. Anger formed like a blanket over the studio as various people jumped up and shouted comments. They wanted the perpetrator of this crime hung! Shot! Strangled!

The man tried to continue telling his story and explained that he called the police in, and the criminal was caught. Even so, another person in the audience jumped up and said, "This criminal should be castrated!"

Then this man being interviewed was asked if he were not extremely angry, and wanted to kill the criminal. This man calmly gave a simple answer. He said, "Vengeance is the Lord's."

Wanting to get even with someone, or seek revenge, is probably one of the most common sinful traits of the human being.

God's teaching clearly states that this is a wrong attitude on our part. In the book of Romans, we read that we are not to repay one evil for another evil. We are not to be overcome by evil, but we are to overcome evil with good. It is God's place to administer judgment, and it is our place and responsibility to serve others in love (Romans 12:19-20).

140

Expression: **Wash my hands of the whole thing**

Location: Matthew 27:24

Verse: When Pilate saw that he could prevail nothing, but that rather a tumult [riot] was made, he took water, and washed his hands before the multitude, saying, I am innocent of the blood of this just person: see ye to it.

"I am sick of it. I wash my hands of the whole thing." When we hear someone use this expression, we easily could think of both Macbeth and Pontius Pilate. These probably are the two most famous cases of one wanting to "wash my hands of the whole thing."

In Shakespeare's tragedy, Lady Macbeth's actual words are, "Go get some water, and wash this filthy witness from your hand." Macbeth asks, "... Will all great Neptune's ocean wash this blood clean from my hand?"

Later Lady Macbeth says, "... Retire we to our chamber. A little water clears us of this deed."

Early in the morning of the day Jesus was crucified, all the chief priests and the elders of the people came to the decision that Jesus should be put to death. They bound him, led him away, and turned him over to Pontius Pilate, the governor.

Pilate could see no fault in Jesus. Pilate knew that it was out of unbelief and envy that the people had turned Jesus over to him. Pilate wanted to release Jesus, but the pressure of the crowd was too overpowering. Pilate decided to wash his hands of the whole thing.

141

Expression: We came in with nothing

Location: 1 Timothy 6:7

Verse: For we brought nothing into this world, and it is certain we can carry nothing out.

During the Golden Age of Radio, there was a quiz program on the air called *Take It or Leave It*. The quizmaster was the comedian and accordion-playing Phil Baker. The top prize for contestants answering the questions correctly was $64. Everyone gathered around the radio each week to hear Phil's humor and the nervous contestants try to answer the questions.

The questions were arranged along a $1, $2, $4, $8, $16, $32, and $64 progression. Contestants could stop answering questions anywhere along the way and take the money, or they could continue on. However, if they continued and missed the answer to a question, they lost everything and went home with nothing.

All of the listeners were intrigued by two responses on just about every show. When a contestant wanted to go on to the next question, we would sit and wait for the studio audience to scream out, "you'll be sorrr-eee!" The second thing we would hear on just about every program was the contestant saying, "I came in with nothing; I might as well leave with nothing."

This expression is even more interesting in that almost these exact words are found in the Bible. The apostle Paul warned Timothy, a young preacher, of many things to be aware of in his preaching and in the leading of his congregation.

Paul is telling Timothy to be content and satisfied with his lot in the will of God.

142

Expression: **Whatever you do, do it the best you can**

Location: Ecclesiastes 9:10

Verse: Whatsoever thy hand findeth to do, do it with thy might....

"Whatever you do, do it the best you can"   is advice which might be given by the parent to the child. This wonderful advice is given by the teacher to the student. This expression could be said to the athlete by the coach.

There is nothing wrong with this expression and this advice. However, seeing it appear in the book of Ecclesiastes makes us think on the whole subject more. When studying the book of Ecclesiastes, we must keep several points in mind.

Solomon is considered by many to be the writer. Solomon also wrote most of the book of Proverbs. In Proverbs we see the wisdom of Solomon and how life ought to be if everyone acted fairly. But in Ecclesiastes we see what often happens in this imperfect world around us. In Ecclesiastes we read about human philosophy apart from God. People try to be happy without God, but this book shows the absurdity of the attempt. We learn that without God we cannot be satisfied. Worldly things cannot satisfy the heart.

The key word in Ecclesiastes is "vanity." This writing comes to conclusions which human beings reach through their own intelligence or experiments.

This expression which we find in Ecclesiastes is good on its own. But read what follows the expression: "... for there is no work, nor device [thought], nor knowledge, nor wisdom, in the grave, whither thou goest" (Ecclesiastes 9:10).

It is certainly true that the body lying in the grave can no longer write books, read books, use computers, or build houses. Solomon is speaking only of the body. In fact, he says, "Whatsoever thy *hand* findeth to do...." He is not talking about the soul. The hand will go in the grave, but if we are a child of God, our soul will go into the presence of our Lord.

143

Expression: When the ox is in the ditch

Location: Luke 14:5

Verse: ... Which of you shall have an ass [donkey] or an ox fallen into a pit, and will not straightway pull him [it] out on the sabbath day?

As a small child and throughout life I have heard the expression about getting the ox out of the ditch. When a person had to work on the Sabbath, someone would say, "Well, when this ox is in the ditch...." As a small child, I was able to figure out that this gave a person reason to work on the Sabbath. (Of course, I feel that the rationalization was often abused, too!)

When I became older, sure enough, there it was in the Bible. I read the words. It is in the book of Luke.

The Revised Standard Version, the New International Version, and other translations of the Bible use the word "son" in place of "donkey." In the book of Deuteronomy, the law is specified for both humans and animals.

The scripture refers to the particular Sabbath day when Jesus went to eat in the house of a prominent Pharisee. Jesus was being carefully watched. Pharisees were teachers in the synagogues and self-appointed guardians of the law and its proper observance. The majority of these "scribes" belonged to the party of the Pharisees.

On this Sabbath day in question, there appeared a man suffering from dropsy. The man's appearing probably was staged by the Pharisees to try to trap Jesus. Jesus asked the Pharisees if it were lawful to heal on the Sabbath or not. By asking them before the miracle, Jesus made it more difficult for them to protest afterward.

After Jesus asked the question, the Pharisees remained silent. So Jesus healed the man with dropsy and sent him away. Then Jesus asked them: "... If one of you has a child or an ox that has fallen into a well, will you not immediately pull it out on a Sabbath day?" (Luke 14:5 NRSV). The Pharisees had nothing to say.

144

Expression: Where your treasure is, there your heart will be also

Location: Matthew 6:21

Verse: For where your treasure is, there your heart will be also.

The congressman voted in support of what would enhance his own position instead of what would be best for the country. The insurance salesman explained a policy to an elderly person so that he could sell the policy and earn the commission rather than tell the truth. The employee in a financial institution misrepresented facts, cheated, and withheld information which enabled her to climb up the corporate ladder in the company.

The congressman's heart was in gaining power. The insurance salesman's heart was in gaining money. The financier's heart was in gaining career advancement.

One of the ten commandments is a warning against covetousness. A covetous person is one who has an inordinate desire for wealth or possessions, or for another's possessions.

In the New Testament, Jesus preaches his Sermon on the Mount to his disciples (Matthew 5-7). The primary purpose of the Sermon on the Mount is to set before us the law of the Kingdom of God.

Jesus teaches not to store up treasures on earth where they can be destroyed, but let our treasures be in heaven where they will never lose their value. Jesus stresses that if our most loved treasures are in heaven, then our hearts are going to be there also. Instead of having our primary thought on material wealth, our primary thought and our love should be in working toward the Kingdom of God.

145

Expression: **A whisperer separates the best of friends**

Location: Proverbs 16:28

Verse: A froward [perverse] man [human being] soweth strife: and a whisperer separateth chief [the best of] friends.

A college senior told of his experience of working in an office for one full summer. To earn money for college, he usually took what he called outside jobs.

He stated that the thing he could vividly remember about that full summer of office work was the close, threatened environment of a small office with three desks. He occupied one desk, and two young ladies probably in their late twenties occupied the other two desks.

This student related that he usually worked quietly, trying to get the paperwork done. These two young ladies apparently had had some gross differences in the past, because their "catty" remarks to each other were persistent throughout the day. He could detect jealousy, spite, vanity, strife, and pure meanness between them.

One day another female worker from another office came by to see one of these women in the office. The two talked to each other quietly. They whispered some. Then on occasion they would burst out in laughter. One would cup her hand to the side of her mouth and say things that no one else was to hear.

The other young lady working in the office became outraged. She presumed that they were talking about her. They were whispering and sometimes giving her smirkish looks. Finally, the young lady, thinking it was secrets about her, ran crying from the office.

From this incident, we might reflect on this verse from Proverbs. The verse says it so well. Chapter 16 of Proverbs blatantly states that a gossip will destroy the best of friends.

Remember, we can't hurt others without hurting ourselves worse. The Bible teaches us a far better way to live.

146

Expression: A widow's mite

Location: Mark 12:42

Verse: And there came a certain poor widow, and she threw in [to the offering box] two mites, which make a farthing.

A neighbor was heard saying, "That dear lady lived on a widow's mite, but still she gave her heart and her mite to the Mission House. Her widow's mite was a tremendous service."

The person describing this woman was referring to the widow's mite that Jesus spoke of in the Bible. A mite is a very small amount of money, but this financial gift is tremendous when it is given through love and self-sacrifice.

Jesus sat in the Temple near the offering box and watched the people put in their money offering. Rich people were able to give large sums of money. The poor widow gave a farthing. A farthing was a coin equal to about one-fourth of a U.S. penny.

Jesus called his disciples and told them that this dear widow had put in more than all the others. Jesus said that the others gave out of their surplus wealth. But this poor widow, out of her poverty, had put in everything she had — all she had to live on. She gave her whole being to God.

147

Expression: **Wisdom is more precious than jewels**

Location: Proverbs 3:15

Verse: She [wisdom] is more precious than rubies.

The music director in a church was seated in a restaurant for lunch with his pastor. They were meeting to discuss some very important issues with regard to the music program.

While they were seated there, two ladies from their church came over to their table. One of the ladies seemed to be especially excited to see them. She said that she had just called the church to speak to the pastor. She needed to meet with him right away about a serious problem that had arisen in her immediate family. Her words addressed to the pastor were, "Next to the wisdom of Solomon, you have the greatest wisdom in helping people with their needs of any person I ever knew."

That was quite a compliment. Before the music director even gave thought to what he said, he quoted the age-old proverb, "One of wisdom is more precious than jewels."

Proverbs 3, verse 13, states that happy is the person that finds wisdom. We may alter that and say, "Happy is the person who finds God's wisdom for daily living." Then Proverbs 3 goes on to say that wisdom is more precious than rubies.

The Bible explains that learning of the wisdom of God is open to everyone. The ways of wisdom are the ways of pleasantness, happiness, faith, and peace.

148

Expression: **With God all things are possible**

Location: Mark 10:27

Verse: And Jesus looking upon them saith, With men [mortals] it is impossible, but not with God: for with God all things are possible.

I have had the opportunity to compose music for choirs during my thirty-year tenure as a minister of music in churches. In one of my musicals called *Spirit of Love*, I composed a song with the title, "For with God, Nothing Will Be Impossible."

After many weeks of rehearsing and finally performing this musical for a worship service, one of the choir members came up to me and said, "Do you know what piece of the musical I like the best?" I was anxious to hear her answer.

This particular choir member was a lovely lady who had often shared with my wife and me the many heartaches and problems she had endured. Her husband died, and she was having many problems with her children. Some of the problems that she related to us would break our hearts to hear as we tried to give her support.

She said, "The song that touched my heart the most is 'For with God, Nothing Will Be Impossible.'"

I was quite gratified that this had meant something to her and had uplifted her spirit in being reminded that God indeed is there to help us through anything and give us comfort.

The most forthright statement of this expression in the Bible is in the book of Luke when the angel appears to Mary, a virgin, and says that she will conceive in her womb, and bring forth a son who shall be called Jesus who will save his people from their sins. For with God nothing shall be impossible (Luke 1:37).

149

Expression: Woe is me!

Location: Psalm 120:5

Verse: Woe is me, that I sojourn [dwell] in Mesech, that I dwell in the tents of Kedar!

Years ago during the Golden Age of Radio, there was a comedian by the name of Joe Penner who got his own show on CBS in 1933 after he had became famous on the *Rudy Vallee Show*. Joe Penner had several trademark sayings such as, "Do you wanna buy a duck?" Another trademark saying of his was, "Woe is me." It is only normal to hear others give out with this expression also when they meet head-on with some kind of trouble.

"Woe" as defined by a dictionary will probably associate the meaning with such words as grief, sorrow, misery, affliction, and trouble.

Mesech and Kedar were remote regions of Asia Minor and northern Arabia. The people of Mesech and Kedar were haters of the Lord and hated peace. The pilgrim in Psalm 120 was for peace, but his voice to the others was unheeded. The pilgrim prayed to the Lord as he exclaimed, "Woe is me."

150

Expression: **Wolves in sheep's clothing**

Location: Matthew 7:15

Verse: Beware of false prophets [teachers], which come to you in sheep's clothing, but inwardly they are ravening [hungry] wolves.

False prophets or teachers were common in Old Testament biblical times. The teachers often spoke what the king and the people wanted to hear. Of course, they claimed that it was God's message. False teachers are plentiful in our day and time also.

Jesus is saying to beware of these teachers whose words sound religious, being disguised as harmless sheep, but who are telling a false gospel. They are really like a wolf which will do harm to you. Beware of wolves in sheep's clothing.

151

Expression: You are the salt of the earth

Location: Matthew 5:13

Verse: Ye are the salt of the earth: but if the salt have lost his [its] savor [flavor], wherewith [how] shall it be salted [seasoned]? It is thenceforth [then] good for nothing, but to be cast [thrown] out, and to be trodden [trampled] under foot of [by] men [people].

One summer we turned on our television sets to watch one of the national political party conventions in session when they nominated their candidate for the Presidency of the United States. This forum allowed opportunities for some to speak out on their views as well as to serve as inciters, thus building enthusiasm among their fellow party members.

On this particular occasion, a speaker was properly introduced with cheering and applause. He stepped up to the podium, and the first words out of his mouth directed to his party members were, "You are the salt of the earth." This brought on at least ten minutes of unabandoned cheering and screaming.

This politician actually spoke words from the Bible. Jesus did not speak these words to receive cheers. He was saying in Matthew 5 that those who really repent of their sins become both "the salt of the earth" and "the light of the world."

One day Jesus went with his disciples up on a hillside and taught them. Jesus delivered his dynamic Sermon on the Mount. He told his disciples that they were the salt of the earth, the world's seasoning, the preserver.

People who strive to be the salt of the earth have an influence for good in the world.

152

Expression: You can't take it with you

Location: 1 Timothy 6:7 (NRSV)

Verse: ... for we brought nothing into the world, so that we can take nothing out of it.

I love to watch the old movies from the Golden Age of Hollywood. The year 1938 is an excellent representative year of that golden era. Some important movie releases of 1938 included Walt Disney's *Snow White and the Seven Dwarfs*; the new star William Holden in *Golden Boy*; Tyrone Power, Alice Faye, and Don Ameche in *Alexander's Ragtime Band* as well as *In Old Chicago*. Bette Davis won her second Oscar for her performance in *Jezebel*, and Frank Capra won his third Oscar for directing *You Can't Take It With You*.

We recently got to see again *You Can't Take It With You* starring Lionel Barrymore, Jimmy Stewart, and Spring Byington. The entertainment value is wonderful. One can sit and reflect on its meaning in a very spiritual way.

The Bible doesn't use the exact words of this often-used expression, "You can't take it with you." However, the scripture indeed does say this in 1 Timothy 6:7.

The message is that we are to use our earthly talents and our money to serve God's purposes. No, we can't take it with us.

153

Expression: You will have to give account for every idle word you speak

Location: Matthew 12:36

Verse: But I say unto you, That every idle [careless] word that men [people] shall speak, they shall give account thereof in the day of judgment.

Little Tommy was angry at his ten-year-old playmate. Tommy's anger stretched his vocabulary to such a height that he was calling his friend every bad name he could think of and accusing him of every bad deed he could imagine.

Needless to say, Tommy's mother, upon hearing this explosive language, called him down and said, "You will have to give account for every idle word you speak."

Over the years, many parents have used this expression directed to their children when they have heard bad or idle talk coming from their mouths.

This expression, which is in the Bible, has a little different meaning from what was thought by many of those parents. In Matthew, chapter 12, Jesus speaks these words.

Jesus explains that we can be forgiven of every sin but one. Jesus says that we cannot be forgiven for blasphemy against the Holy Spirit. This is the unpardonable sin. (See Matthew 12:31-32.)

Blasphemy against the Holy Spirit is rejection of the Holy Spirit, thereby not receiving forgiveness, therefore not receiving salvation.

"Idle words" mentioned in Matthew 12:36 are connected to the unpardonable sin. Jesus tells us that our words as well as our acts show off our character. For by our words we shall be justified, and by our words we shall be condemned (Matthew 12:37).

154

Expression: **Your labor is not in vain**

Location: 1 Corinthians 15:58

Verse: Therefore, my beloved brethren, be ye steadfast, unmov-
able, always abounding in the work of the Lord, forasmuch
as ye know [knowing] that your labor is not in vain in the
Lord.

Recently I had the privilege of teaching a class one night a
week to the very fine young people at a local Christian college.

One night I heard two young men running in the hall and stumbling up the stairs just outside the room I was using. One of them
said as he ran, completely overcome with excitement, "We're doing the work of the Lord."

I don't have the slightest idea as to what the two young people
were doing. I was very impressed that two young people were so
excited about whatever their project was that one would want to
say to the other as they ran, "We're doing the work of the Lord."

Chapter 15 of First Corinthians closes with the apostle Paul
telling his beloved church members that their eventual victory is
assured if they remain strong and steadfast, always working for the
Lord. The scripture promises us that our labor is not in vain in the
Lord.

AND, God keeps promises!